After the Storm

ABOUT THIS BOOK

What you have in your hand is really two books in one.

The first book, Helping Your Family During a Crisis, *is a concise set of directions for stabilizing your family in an emergency. Use this Emergency Guide when confronted with an emotional crisis like the aftermath of an experience of violence or a natural disaster.*

The second book, After the Storm, *is a guide to help you understand and deal with the long-term stress that follows difficult events. Using real-life examples, it explains why people often hurt and are not fully functional for months or even years after a crisis. It gives suggestions for self-help for those in pain. It also covers some of the theory and research underlying the Emergency Guide.*

We need more than wrenches, flashlights, and duct tape to deal with major crisis and disaster. Our ability to respond to the immediate situation can be sabotaged by our own panic, rage, and hysteria, or by the reactions of those around us. Later, we face the task of adjusting to the new conditions brought about by the crisis. Still later we, and those we love, may suffer delayed reactions that reduce our ability to recover, destroy our health, and damage our relationships.

The two parts of this book will give you resources to stabilize yourself and your family during a trauma, tragedy, or terror, and to start the healing afterward.

About the Author

Kendall Johnson, Ph.D., serves as a crisis-management consultant to several major school districts nationwide and teaches in the Claremont Unified School District in Claremont, Southern California. He is a twenty-five-year veteran classroom teacher, has served as a mentor teacher, and is NBPTS board certified in adolescent/young adult art. In addition, he is a licensed marriage and family therapist specializing in posttrauma issues and has trained school crisis-response teams for over twenty years.

Dr. Johnson serves in an advisory capacity to the Psychological Trauma Center, Los Angeles; Harlem Hospital, New York City; Walter Reed Army Medical Center, Washington DC; and Mercy Corps. He serves on the faculty of the International Critical Incident Stress Foundation and on the editorial board of the *International Journal of Emergency Mental Health.*

In addition to journal articles and training materials, Dr. Johnson has written numerous books on the themes of trauma, crisis, and recovery for mental-health professionals, school personnel, and parents. His works include:*Trauma in the Lives of Children; Responding to School Crisis: A CISM Approach; School Crisis Management: A Hands-On Guide to Training Crisis Response Teams, Classroom Crisis: The Teacher's Guide; Turning Yourself Around: Self-Help Strategies for Troubled Teens;* and *Reclaiming Your Future.* He has also coauthored several workbooks in the Growth and Recovery Workbook (GROW) series published by Hunter House for counselors and therapists working with children who have experienced disabling trauma and loss.

TO CONTACT THE AUTHOR

Kendall Johnson can be reached for consultation or training at (909) 626-2207 or at kjohnson@chsmail.claremont.edu.

Praise for the author's earlier books

TRAUMA IN THE LIVES OF CHILDREN

"Ultimately, *Trauma in the Lives of Children* is about helping youngsters recover from overwhelming stress and it contains a remarkable synthesis of useful tehchniques.... [A]s this book so well documents, we can offer effective help to our young patients, their families and their schools in the afttermath of trauma. This work must be given priority attention both because of the prevalence of PTSD and because of its responsiveness to therapeutic intervention. Dr. Kendall Johnson, master teacher and thera-pist, is to be congratulated on an important contribution to the mental health literature. *Trauma in the Lives of Children* deserves to be read by every professional who cares for children in our troubled world."

— *Spencer Eth, M.D.*, Associate Chief of Psychiatry,
Veterans Administration Medical Center, Los Angeles

SCHOOL CRISIS MANAGEMENT

"*School Crisis Management* fills a huge gap in the literature on traumatic events that affect children and adolescents. It leaps forward from the theoretical and plants itself firmly as a benchmark for realistic crisis inter-vention programs in the school systems of English-speaking countries. It should not be long before the book is translated into other languages."

— *Jeffrey T. Mitchell, Ph.D.*, President, International Critical Incident
Stress Foundation; Clinical Associate Professor of Emergency Health
Services, The University of Maryland, Baltimore County

"Kendall Johnson's book fills a gap that has been waiting to be bridged between theory and practice. This important contribution will be welcomed by teachers and educationists around the world—both for its accessible information on posttrauma psychology and the understanding of the prac-tical needs of busy classroom teachers. It will give them the confidence to take on their vital role in reducing stress on their pupils following a trau-matic event."

— *Elizabeth Capewell, M.A.*, Director, Centre for
Crisis Management and Education, England

Praise for the author's earlier books

CLASSROOM CRISIS: THE TEACHER'S GUIDE

"On September 11, after the terrorist attacks on New York and Washington, DC, requests for the booklet began pouring into the central office from schools at every level. More than 1,000 booklets were put into LBUSD teachers' hands in those first hours alone. The booklet has been praised by teachers as being extremely user-friendly—the perfect tool to help children at the classroom level during and after crises. It is easy to understand and easy to use.

"Kendall Johnson is one of the foremost international experts on the topic of school crisis response. He uses his tremendous grasp of the subject to transform complex ideas into a simple and understandable resource. *Classroom Crisis* gives teachers thoughtful and practical answers to the question, 'But what do I do?' It also gives great guidelines for knowing when children need additional help. If there is one book that a teacher needs for dealing with the unthinkable, this is it."

— *Joanne Tortorici Luna, Ph.D.,* Professor of Educational Psychology, California State University, Long Beach, Crisis Team Leader, Long Beach Unified School District

"Seldom does a practitioner in the area of trauma resolution speak to the heart and soul of healing as Kendall Johnson has done with his new book. This contribution to the literature is easy to read, and the vivid examples illuminate the often dark recesses of resolving loss, grief, and trauma....

"After my professional efforts at the Pentagon on 9-11 involving significant exposure and fatigue, who was I going to turn to? Kendall became my support and debriefer—the traumatologist healer! It is because of his depth of caring, creativity, and scholarship that many persons have been assisted in dealing with the life-changing, charged, and churning challenges that loss/grief and trauma bring."

— *Victoria Bruner, LCSW,* Walter Reed Army Medical Center

ORDERING

Trade bookstores in the U.S. and Canada please contact:

Publishers Group West
1700 Fourth Street, Berkeley CA 94710
Phone: (800) 788-3123   Fax: (510) 528-3444

Hunter House books are available at bulk discounts for textbook course adoptions; to qualifying community, health-care, and government organizations; and for special promotions and fund-raising. For details please contact:

Special Sales Department
Hunter House Inc., PO Box 2914, Alameda CA 94501-0914
Phone: (510) 865-5282   Fax: (510) 865-4295
E-mail: ordering@hunterhouse.com

Individuals can order our books from most bookstores, by calling **(800) 266-5592**, or from our website at **www.hunterhouse.com**

PROJECT CREDITS

Cover Design: Brian Dittmar Graphic Design
Book Production: Hunter House
Developmental and Copy Editors: Kelley Blewster, Elaine Ratner, Kiran Rana
Editorial Assistance: Claire Reilly Shapiro
Proofreader: John David Marion
Indexer: Nancy D. Peterson
Acquisitions Editor: Jeanne Brondino
Editor: Alexandra Mummery
Publicist: Jillian Steinberger
Customer Service Manager: Christina Sverdrup
Order Fulfillment: Washul Lakdhon
Administrator: Theresa Nelson
Computer Support: Peter Eichelberger
Publisher: Kiran S. Rana

After the Storm

Kendall Johnson, Ph.D.

book one

Helping Your Family During a Crisis
An Emergency Guide

STARTS ON PAGE **1**
USE THIS IF YOU AND YOUR FAMILY ARE IN A CRISIS SITUATION.
IT IS DESIGNED TO HELP IMMEDIATELY.

book two

After the Storm
Healing after Trauma, Tragedy and Terror

STARTS ON PAGE **37**
READ THIS TO UNDERSTAND MORE ABOUT WHY CRISES
AND DIFFICULT EVENTS LEAVE LASTING SCARS. FIND OUT
WHAT YOU CAN DO TO FEEL BETTER.

HunterHouse PUBLISHERS

Hunter House Inc., Publishers
PO Box 2914
Alameda CA 94501-0914

LIBRARY OF CONGRESS CATALOGING-IN-PUBLICATION DATA
Johnson, Kendall, 1945–
After the storm : healing after trauma, tragedy and terror / Kendall Johnson.
p. cm.
Includes bibliographical references and index.
ISBN-13: 978-0-89793-474-9 (pbk.)
ISBN 10: 0-89793-474-1 (pbk.)
1. Stress management. 2. Psychic trauma. 3. Post-traumatic stress disorder. I. Title.
RA785.J646 2003
616.85'21—dc21   2003012854

Printed and bound by Bang Printing, Brainerd, Minnesota

Manufactured in the United States of America

9 8 7 6 5 4 3 2 1   First Edition   06 07 08 09 10

Helping Your Family During a Crisis

An Emergency Guide

Emergency situations create intense stress. This stress affects how we see things and how we respond. Emergency stress reactions can affect the behavior of both individuals and groups. Incidents or situations that can trigger stress reactions include

- *personal crisis, such as a painful social encounter, an assault, or an accident*
- *crisis events at school or in the community, including news of war or terror*
- *natural disaster*
- *confinement at home during a community emergency*
- *exposure to others' injuries or suffering*
- *evacuation or displacement from home*

You can manage your own and family members' reactions, but first there are a few things you need to know. You need to know how to size up your own or another's response level, how to identify the two general response patterns to extreme stress, and what to do to manage each. You then need to know how to handle the whole family, particularly when some members are reacting poorly. Finally, you need to know how to support family members afterward. The good news—and it is very good news—is that these tools for hope are fairly simple, straightforward, and powerful.

1

Contents

How Crises Affect Us

Crises are events that overwhelm an individual's capacity to cope. They also usually have a negative effect on family behavior. They can be destabilizing, causing emotional problems, confused thinking, and behavioral changes. A person's recovery after a crisis is determined in part by whether he or she is close to supportive, caring people who help him or her to deal with the experience.

On the morning of September 11, 2001, families across the United States awoke to a changed world. Terrorism took on new meaning and a personal face. As the initial moments of shock gave way to the realization of what had actually happened, millions of parents turned to their confused, badly shaken children and, whether they were trained to deal with trauma or not, had to decide what to do and what to say.

Since that day we seem to have been blitzed with a series of major events that continue to shake us. Terrorists have struck civilian targets in Europe, Asia, and the Middle East. Natural disasters have been compounded by human error. The wars in Iraq and Afghanistan seemed to many to invite further violence and hostility toward the United States. Everyone seems to live their lives waiting for the next shoe to drop.

We are all painfully aware that further terrorist attacks may occur at any time, as may other catastrophes, from school shootings to natural disasters. But it doesn't take a terrorist strike or a natural disaster to create crisis in the home. Against a backdrop of pervasive anxiety, the normal range of human crisis takes on new meaning: Reactions to the sudden loss of family members, accidents, or victimization become more intense and destabilizing because everyone's resilience is weakened.

In these turbulent times all families need strategies and resources—practical tools—to help them cope with emergencies. This Emergency Guide presents the tools you need in a usable format. It is not a manual that will teach you how to hang plastic sheeting or store water. It offers you direction for stabilizing your loved ones' emotional reactions and shows how you can provide follow-up support. It is not intended to train you to be a psychotherapist but rather to help you take care of your family more effectively.

How to Use this Guide

In an emergency—be it school violence or a hurricane, a fire in your home, or a serious accident—you can take steps to stabilize your crisis and speed your own and your family's recovery. The tools in this Emergency Guide are coping techniques gathered from fire lines, police debriefings, military preparation, large-scale catastrophes, and community disasters, then sharpened through field application, clinical work, and review.

Read through this Guide and learn how to use the tools it contains. They are the same tools I teach to crisis teams, first responders, and mental-health professionals, nationally and internationally. They will help you to manage your own reactions in an emergency, and also to stabilize those around you. As you move forward after the crisis, they will enable you to shake off the lasting effects of crisis and to renew your spirit and sense of direction.

Important Note: This Guide is in no way intended to substitute for qualified psychological therapy or consultation. You should take advantage of help from mental-health professionals when it is available.

YOUR NOTES

_____

_____

_____

_____

_____

_____

_____

_____

_____

_____

The Basics of Dealing with Crisis

1. Learn to Intervene (Help) Effectively

Intervening—helping—in an effective, caring way following a crisis can minimize the negative effects on individuals and groups. In addition, the process of helping is a tremendous team builder, and can create a sense of cohesiveness and belonging in a family, school, or other group. By reading this guide you are learning to help in a crisis.

2. Recognize the Effects of Crisis

To help others, you need to have a basic understanding of how crises affect them. A crisis always creates instability. A family is a close-knit group and any event that affects one family member affects the others. Shared difficulties can bring the family together or pull it apart. When family members help each other, the whole family can be more easily stabilized.

Acute Stress Response. In a crisis, some family members are able to function and to respond positively, others may be overwhelmed. They may overreact (become agitated) or underreact (shut down). Both these reactions are forms of *acute stress response (ASR)* that make it difficult to think, feel, and act. For more information on acute stress response, see Chapter 3 of the main text. For methods of dealing with acute stress response, see Chapter 8.

Delayed Stress Response. Sometimes the effects of a crisis do not surface for weeks, months, or even years. This is called a *delayed stress response.* It is thought that delayed stress response happens when the strategies used to cope with a critical incident prevent emotional processing of the event. Later, memories and feelings about the incident emerge, causing distress and further attempts at coping. Both temporary problems at the time of crisis and delayed problems can later escalate into serious disorders, such as anxiety or depressive syndromes, dissociation, or even posttraumatic stress disorder. For more information about delayed stress response and posttraumatic stress disorder, see Chapters 5 and 6 of the main text.

3. Take Action, Protect Your Family

Our first job in the face of personal crisis and social uncertainty is to protect and stabilize those around us. An old television advertisement promoted toothpaste by alluding to an "invisible shield." A transparent barrier stood between the user's teeth and the threat of cavities. In much the same way, children or dependent adults in healthy homes feel protected from threat by their parents' and caregivers' presence and care. This shield stands between them and harm.

Adults have learned to anticipate danger. They take action in defense of those they care for. Partners and spouses help each other around harmful events and reassure each other that everything will turn out all right. When things do go wrong and pets or people die, when frightening events occur or grandparents are hurt, parents soothe their children's fears, ease the pain, and get things back to normal as quickly as possible.

This is what those we care for need and expect from us. They need us to give them the freedom to grow when it's safe, but to circle the wagons when threats are present.

4. Reach Out for Support

If you are dealing with an individual or family crisis, there is support available in the community. Books abound, and so do support groups. Public and private agencies offer assistance. Some professionals specialize in dealing with crisis and personal difficulty. (See Chapter 12 of *After the Storm* for a discussion of issues to consider when choosing a mental-health professional.) If the crisis you're dealing with is community-wide, such help will be spread thin for a while. Be assured that many other families are going through the same circumstances. Reach out to them and share resources.

5. Look after Yourself

If you have children, a dependent partner or spouse, or elderly or diabled people in your family, they will look to you for protection. That means it's essential that you manage your own reactions to the threat or crisis. The "How to Stabilize Yourself" section in this Guide can help you do that. Chapter 8 of the main text offers more strategies on centering your thoughts, emotions, and behavior when they threaten to spiral out of control or shut down entirely. Finally, keep reading. The next section will help you prepare yourself and your family for crisis.

Preparing for Crisis

Stabilization begins at home. The planning and preparation you do now will set the stage for effective action during an emergency. Much of your family's ability to remain calm during a crisis will depend upon how well each family member has thought through your plans.

Each emergency may be unique, but the background against which it takes place defines it. A child being dropped off at school may have more trouble with separation anxiety if her father has just been deployed overseas. Every incident—large or small—gains energy and meaning from its context. For instance, the words "I do" mean very different things when said in response to the question "Who wants the hamburger?" and when spoken in church in front of a minister and potential spouse. When uncertainty about safety and the ecnomony permeates our communities and our homes, it colors any crisis—personal or community-wide—that comes along.

Preparing Your Children

Nobody likes crisis, least of all our children. They see that the adults around them are upset, but they often have no idea why. They have no way to assess how bad things are or whether they themselves will be all right. Frightening events mix with kids' lack of understanding to make normal dependency worse.

Finding new sources of support for your children during hard times may be challenging. The more children can talk about what they feel, the better they understand their feelings. Children know when their parents are upset but few children can relate to abstract concepts like "global terrorism,"and lectures on political instability will only confuse and frighten them. What they need to know is that their parents will be there to help. We can begin the process of stabilization by opening channels of communication so that fears can be expressed and understood.

Talking to Your Children

It's hard to know what to tell our children in times of crisis. Old platitudes like "everything will be fine" ring hollow to us and probably won't comfort them. Talk about world events or local crises with your children. They will hear about them whether you talk about them or not, on television, in school, and from friends. When you talk about world events at home, you can keep in touch with how your children see things. What you learn may be surprising sometimes, but it will give you the direction you need to help stabilize them.

Just as every family is different, so is every conversation. There is no set protocol for talking with our children about fearful events but a few helpful guidelines are listed below. (For information about talking to kids during or after an actual emergency or crisis, see the section in the main text, Chapter 11, titled "How to Talk to Children After a Crisis: An Example.") The guidelines that follow are general suggestions to use when talking to any family members about difficult matters that concern them, including global or community events.

1. Start by listening, not telling
You probably have lots of opinions about how the world got this way and what can go wrong next. Rather than leading with your opinions, begin by finding out what your children understand about the situation and how they think and feel about it. The conversation should be about *their* fears, anger, and concerns, not yours.

2. Use words they can understand
Understand the limits of their comprehension and communication. Big words like *globalization, national security*, or *preemptive war* mean very little to children, even to younger adolescents. Break it down for them, and then, by listening, you can find out what triggers their feelings.

3. Listen to the fears hidden behind their words
As you talk about their concepts and ideas about what is happening, gently seek out what lies beneath—the things they imagine might happen, their worries, and their fears for their well-being. Look for the concern that remains unspoken, and help bring it to light.

4. Keep your own fears in check
Your children want to hear words of comfort, but they also look for warning signs. They know to look to actions first, words second. If you say "Everything is fine," and you are taking another drink, smoking a cigarette, yelling at your spouse, and tapping your foot compulsively, your children see right through you. A constricted voice and shaking hands telegraph the real message. As a way of managing your own fears, read and practice the processes included in Chapter 8 of the main text for recentering your thoughts, emotions, and physical reactions to a more positive state.

5. Aim for clarity

Figure out what your children are really asking by posing questions. Watch their body language. Ask for examples if you are still unclear. Look for ways in which your children may be confused and ways in which their confusion may be increasing their anxiety. Straighten out their muddles, using language and concepts they can understand.

6. Provide reassurance

Remember the bottom line: Children need to know that the parental protective shield is still up. Don't get caught up in media hype and political jargon. Stay focused on the present. Instead of talking about what could happen, spend comfortable time together. Let your children know that they are the central focus in your life by doing things with them, enjoying your time together, and demonstrating your love.

7. Coordinate your efforts with your spouse or other adults.

Taking care of your children involves planning and coordination with other adults: your spouse or significant other, your kids' other parent if the two of you no longer live together, extended family in the household or nearby, and any other adults that play a role in the life of your family. Make sure you work closely with each involved adult before, during, and after crisis.

Preparing Yourself

Your ability to keep your family calm during a crisis depends more upon your state of mind and readiness than upon external events. Time spent preparing yourself now will pay off for them later. Before a crisis occurs, you can do the following:

Develop awareness of your own vulnerability and limitations

Think about areas where you may be especially sensitive because of prior crises in your life. Be honest with yourself about what kinds of situations you are good at handling and what kinds of situations you need help with.

Realize that you need support; know whom to turn to after an incident

Before a crisis occurs, think through what sorts of assistance you could use in different kinds of situations, and who might be willing to provide it to you. Consider developing a list of people you trust and with whom you could talk should things become difficult. Trusted friends and family members can help you keep perspective and can point out things you may have failed to consider. Let them know that you may be calling on them.

Plan for routine self-care following a crisis
Make a list of the things that keep you healthy. Whether it be exercise, diet, or spiritual activity, plan ways to maintain that care system following an emergency.

Do ongoing work on personal issues that leave you vulnerable
Everybody has personal issues that tend to get worse during periods of stress. Keep working on these issues before a crisis occurs.

Set limits on demands from others and from yourself
As a normal human being, you have limits on your time, energy, and resources. During a crisis, everything is stretched even thinner. Learn how to set limits now so you won't let your own needs or the needs of others leave you totally drained after a crisis.

Learn what to do in different kinds of crises
Different kinds of emergencies require different responses—a fire in your home, for example, requires different responses than the threat of violence at your child's school. The more familiar you are with the specific needs created by emergencies, the greater will be your ability to respond effectively. Emergency guidelines are available from many sources, including the Federal Emergency Management Agency (FEMA) and state offices of emergency service. Contact information for these resources can be found in the Appendix at the end of this Guide.

Learn how people react to emergencies and how to help them
Read the rest of this Emergency Guide, as well as Chapters 3 and 8 in the main text, to familiarize yourself with acute stress reactions and how to manage them.

The best preparation for emergencies is a solid relationship of trust and communication among family members. This takes time to develop, but it pays off when things become difficult.

What to Do when Emergency Strikes

Bad things do happen. When they do, there are many ways you can reduce the impact on your children or others in your care. By taking a few simple actions, you can minimize their panic and reinforce their sense of security. But first you must be aware of your own response level and take steps to stay effective. Use the techniques of breath control, self-talk, and physical-activity level outlined later in this guide to keep yourself functioning. Once you are coping, then turn to helping others.

When emergency strikes, it is time to stabilize the home. Stay informed without creating more of an emergency than already exists. Do what needs to be done, but do it calmly.

1. First, turn off the TV
Put away the news magazines and newspaper headlines, and don't tune into talk radio. Turn away from the media-induced hysteria that creates a sense of constant emergency in the home. Monitor adult conversation as well. You need to talk about what's going on, but your kids will hear your fear, not the facts. When talking to other adults in front of children, stick to essential facts—the things you know for sure, not the things you fear or the speculations you entertain.

2. Follow the course of action dictated by the emergency
Turn the radio or television on for short periods of time when children are not present in order to monitor any directions given by authorities.

3. Listen to newscasts, to stay informed of developments
Caution: Do not become transfixed by continuous news reporting. Turn the radio or TV on periodically for updated information; then, when the news cycle begins to repeat, turn it off. Another caution: Do not allow children to watch the TV until you know it does not present confusing information or distressing images. Local radio usually describes local conditions with less drama than national television does.

4. Observe your children's reactions
Look for signs of extreme distress or detachment. (The signs of acute stress reaction are described in Chapters 3 and 8 of the main text.) Children manifest the same basic range of response as adults, with some differences according to age.

5. Above all, project calm

Go about dealing with the incident in a matter-of-fact manner. If you cannot control your emotions around your children, find someone who can. It's okay to let your kids know something is happening; it's not okay to inflict your emotional overflow on them. Emergency situations are not times for group therapy; they are times for calm, determined leadership.

6. Use the techniques outlined below to help stabilize your family

To recap, you need to know how to evaluate your own or another's response level, how to identify the two general response patterns to extreme stress, and what to do to manage each. You then need to know how to handle the whole family, particularly when some members are reacting poorly. Finally, you need to know how to support family members afterward.

Assess Others' Reactions to the Emergency

Our response, when bad things happen, includes all our thoughts, feelings, and actions. Depending on the situation, these responses can vary from mild to extreme. In the table below, the spectrum of response to a crisis is divided into seven degrees, ranging from complete shutdown to complete loss of control. Each position on the spectrum is named and the typical

A SEVEN-POINT RANGE OF RESPONSE TO CRISIS	
Position on spectrum	*Description*
1. Acute stress shutdown	Unable to respond
2. Faded	Becoming disconnected from the situation and from one's own reactions
3. Objective	Personal involvement is secondary to overall perspective
4. Fully present	Fully aware and focused upon the situation
5. Involved	Some degree of personal involvement and subjectivity
6. Overreactive	Personal involvement overrides broader perspective
7. Acute stress agitation	Unable to control or direct behavior

behavior is described in a little more detail. As we can see, acute stress responses (ASR) show up at both extremes of the spectrum, that is, as acute stress shut down and acute stress agitation.

The next table, below, describes the two response extremes, shutdown and agitation, in more detail. They look very different, in terms of both physical appearance, functioning, and behavior.

THE TWO EXTREMES OF RESPONSE TO CRISIS	
Faded or shutdown	*Overreactive or agitated*
Pale, shocklike appearance	Flushed, sweaty appearance
Submissiveness	Panicked, enraged, or hysterical behavior
Blunted affect, slowed behavior	Rapid, undirected, ineffective action
Extreme: paralysis, immobility	Extreme: uncontrolled behavior

If you recognize any of these reactions in another person or in yourself, it may be wise to intervene or seek assistance. In order to stabilize a situation, you must stabilize the individuals involved.

The two extremes of ASR, agitation and shutdown, have to be dealt with differently but the basic approach to managing them both is common.

— *First,* both must be dealt with at the levels of thoughts, feelings, bodily actions, and behavior.

— *Second,* the goals for intervention are the same, whether the reaction is shutdown or agitation.

— *Third,* start by offering strategies for changing the person's thoughts. How people think about a situation and frame it in their mind are easier to change than their emotions, bodily reactions, or behaviors. Therefore, when intervening in a person's response to crisis, that is the best place to start. In particular, attempt to shift the person's (or your own) focus, self-talk, and mental images. (More about each of these suggestions is given in the tools below.) Then move on to dealing with emotions, bodily reactions, and behavior, in that order.

The table below summarizes of the goals of intervention in ASR:

HANDLING ASR: INTERVENTION LEVELS AND GOALS

Level	Goal
Thoughts	Focus attention
Feelings	Stabilize feelings
Body	Adjust movement, pacing, arousal
Behavior	Direct action

Tools for Dealing with Reactions to an Emergency

The way you approach a person who is in the middle of a crisis affects that person's behavior. It is important to stay calm and positive. Use the following tools—in roughly the order in which they are presented—to help stabilize individuals in crisis. Note that these tools are used in different ways to deal with persons who are agitated and those who are shutting down.

You can use these tools either on yourself or to help someone else. Following the general explanations below are suggestions for stabilizing yourself and then stabilizing your family or others.

Focus
Imagination can fire fears. Work at focusing on the here and now. If you or another person is shutting down, direct attention outward. If you or another person is growing agitated, shift attention back to the self.

Self-Talk/Other Talk
The words we choose to describe things shape our expectations, and our expectations influence our reactions. Use clear language when talking to yourself or others. Don't use extreme or alarming words when normal words will do. Speak in calming ways. Use positive reminders like "Remember to think," "Things will work out," and "Stay focused and stay strong."

Imagery
Mental pictures, which also guide our actions and our responses, can be used to calm ourselves down or push us into action. They can be directly

suggested or simply embedded in conversation. Tell yourself (or another) to visualize positive outcomes.

Feelings

Feelings drive both physical reactions and thought processes. They can be intensified or softened by words and images. You can also summon up alternative sets of feelings by directing attention to different aspects of the situation. Use a calming tone of voice, body posture, and facial expression. If you're talking to someone else, look the person in the eye and hold his or her gaze. Stand directly in front of them as you speak. Describe what you see happening, in order to redirect their attention.

Breath

Both thoughts and physical reactions can be shifted by changing breathing patterns. To reduce agitation, learn and be able to demonstrate the following "four-count breath protocol": Inhale deeply for a count of four ... hold the breath for for a count of four ... then let the breath out slowly for a count of four ... hold it out for a count of four. Repeat the cycle four times. This breathing technique initiates the relaxation response.

Alternatively, to escalate reactions in cases of shutdown, simply take several quick panting breaths ("quick breaths").

Bodily Pacing

To focus thoughts and control feelings, slow down your—or another's— body movements. Alternatively, to mobilize thoughts and get in touch with feelings, pick up the pacing of movements.

Directing Physical Energy

During agitation, the body is jerky and hyperactive. Redirecting body energy to more deliberate, productive tasks allows that energy to dissipate. During shutdown, the body is inert, awaiting direction and conserving energy. Stretching, moving around, and taking purposive action allows the energy to flow again. If you become aware that you are either agitated or fading out, find someone you can accompany, and let their activity guide you. Alternatively, if you are trying to help someone who is agitated or fading, ask the person to accompany you while you are doing things. Walk, move, and speak at a pace similar to the other person's, then gradually slow down if the person is agitated, or speed up if the person is fading. When the person is responding favorably, give him or her an appropriate task to complete.

Action

Find something to do, or give someone you are trying to help something to do. This will help pick up or calm down reaction levels and redirect attention more meaningfully. You can assign simple actions: "Take a walk," or "Sit down." Other actions are more complex: "Take this box to that person." "Organize these papers." "Please pack these lunches." Be sure the activities are within the range of ability of the person at the time. The purpose of the action is twofold: to appropriately direct energy and focus, and to reestablish a sense of control and self-worth.

Ritual

If the crisis lasts over an extended period, use rituals to keep your family and yourself stable. Every family has rituals—activities such as dinners together, family conferences, or going places together. Rituals guide awareness, balance emotions, and focus energy. Some rituals are used to mobilize energy to face challenges. Others bring comfort and a sense of community support. Intentionally use your existing family patterns and routines as rituals during stressful times. Spend time together in meaningful ways in order to allow the sense of family support to help stabilize each family member. Consider creating new rituals for the occasion, such as lighting a candle and sharing thoughts and feelings after supper.

How to Stabilize Yourself

First things first. In order to be able to help others, you must first stabilize your own reactions. If you think you might be agitated or shut-down, you probably are. Take that fact into consideration when you size up the situation. Before you try to help anybody else, pull yourself back to center. This section summarizes how to do this, using the tools described above.

Begin with a self-assessment.

Ask yourself: Am I overreacting or becoming agitated? Consider the following specific questions:

- Is this situation threatening? How much actual threat is there?
- Is the threat from outside me or inside me?
- What is my reaction level (on the seven-point scale)?
- Do I feel fear or anger, or is it panic, rage, or hysteria?
- What does my body tell me?

- Does time seem to be slowing down?

- How are others acting and reacting?

- What might they see that I don't?

- Can I ask them?

- What evidence could I look for to confirm my feelings and reactions?

If you feel you might be overreacting or growing agitated, use the tools in the "Self-Care Actions for Agitation" table below.

SELF-CARE ACTIONS FOR AGITATION	
Tool	*How to use it*
Focus	Ignore memories and imagination; focus on the present
Self-talk/other talk	Use soothing and calming self-talk; talk to others
Imagery, expectations	Visualize a safe place; visualize positive actions and outcomes
Breath	Initiate four-count breathing
Relaxation	Sit down; change scenery
Direction	Find something useful to do; find support and assistance
Activity	Stretch; take a relaxing walk; do a calming ritual

Next, ask yourself: Am I fading out or shutting down?
Consider the following specific questions:

- Do things seem to be slipping out of control and beyond understanding?

- Am I beginning to believe or feel that things just don't seem to matter?

- What is my reaction level (on the seven-point scale)?

- Am I aware of my body?

- Do others seem agitated compared to me?

- Does time seem to be going too fast?
- Are people talking loudly at me, or getting in my face?
- What might they be seeing that I am not?

If you feel you might be underreacting or shutting down, use the tools in the "Self-Care Actions for Shutdown" table below.

SELF-CARE ACTIONS FOR SHUTDOWN	
Tool	*How to use it*
Focus	Ignore memories and imagination; focus on the present
Self-talk/other talk	Use positive, empowering self-talk; speak to others
Imagery, expectations	Visualize positive actions and successful outcomes
Breath	Initiate quick breaths
Arousal	Get up and move; shake it off
Direction	Find something useful to do; find support and assistance
Activity	Take a power walk; exercise; do a strengthening ritual

How to Stabilize Your Family

Once you are functioning, you are in a position to help your family become more stabilized. This section summarizes how to do this, using the tools described earlier. (See also the guidelines in the section in the main text, Chapter 11, titled "How to Talk to Children After a Crisis: An Example.")

Begin by making sure everyone is safe. After that your first priority is to help your family members cope with the emergency and calm their reactions. Show them that they are a unit and can assist and rely upon one another.

During the crisis you should do the following:

- Provide for everyone's physical safety and security.
- Maintain the level of discipline and control you are comfortable with.

- Stay aware of your own response level on the seven-point scale outlined above. This will help you assess the situation.

- Make sure that your own personal issues or fears don't color your evaluation of the situation.

- So that you can remain effective as you help others, continue using the techniques for handling agitation and shutdown on yourself, if necessary.

- Consider obtaining assistance. Get as much help as possible in dealing with the situation.

- Let others help or even take over when necessary.

If time allows, use the following suggestions to provide support to individuals and the family as a whole:

- If the situation allows, engage the family in conversation. This helps reestablish a sense of normalcy and control.

- Ask what they understand about what's happening.

- Try to acknowledge and clarify the thoughts and feelings of the person/people you are helping.

- Show family members through your words and actions that you are trying to help.

- Avoid contradicting their feelings or making false assurances.

- Use active listening. Repeat back what they have told you in order to show them that you have heard. Check out whether you understood by asking, "Is that what you mean?"

- If you think someone's misunderstanding of the situation is making things worse, provide a clearer picture in words they will understand.

- If you feel that family members are beginning to fade, help to refocus them using the techniques described above. Similarly, if they are fearful or overly excited, help them relax.

- As necessary, assist in managing serious reactions. (See the next section, "What to Look Out For," for how to do this.)

- Let people know what's going to happen next, as far as you know.

What to Look Out For

Sometimes emergency behavior goes to greater extremes, warranting immediate referral to medical or mental-health specialists if they are available. Several key signs of acute stress response signal a psychological emergency. These signs fall into three areas: cognitive, emotional, and behavioral.

How They Are Thinking (Cognitive Reactions)

Watch for overfunctioning, underfunctioning, or bizarre thoughts.
Any cognitive reaction may be said to be serious when

- slight disorientation has become an inability to tell one's own name and the date, or relate what has happened over the past twenty-four hours

- too much concern over little things has become an exclusive preoccupation with one idea

- denial of severity has become a wholesale denial that the situation exists

- brief flashbacks have become hallucinations that are out of control

- self-doubt or feelings of unreality have become a "fear of losing one's mind" or an inability to stay in the present

- difficulty in planning has become an inability to carry out basic life functions

- confusion has given way to bizarre, irrational beliefs, and these beliefs form the basis for action

How They Are Feeling (Emotional Reactions)

Watch for emotional extremes that affect functioning.
Any emotional reaction may be said to be serious when

- crying has become uncontrolled hysteria

- anger or self-blame has become fear of or threats of harm to self or others

- blunted feelings have become complete withdrawal with no emotional response

- despair or depression has become self-destructive

How They Are Acting (Behavioral Reactions)

Watch for unfocused agitation, inability to function, or lack of control. *Any behavioral reaction may be said to be serious when*

- restlessness or excitement has become unfocused agitation
- excessive talking or nervousness has become uncontrolled
- frequent retelling of the incident has become continual or ritualistic
- pacing, hand wringing, or clenched fists have become ritualistic or uncontrolled
- withdrawal has become physical immobility or rigidity
- disheveled appearance over time has become an inability to care for oneself
- anger has become destructive or assaultive

The above are signs of extreme stress. If you see them, get medical help. If medical help is unavailable, help to contain the person until it is.

YOUR NOTES

_____

_____

_____

_____

_____

_____

_____

_____

_____

After the Emergency Is Over

Just because the emergency dust has settled, it doesn't mean the crisis is over. Emergencies can terrify and destabilize the entire family. Fortunately, there is some good news. We have learned much over the past few years about children's reactions to crisis, about how multiple exposures to crisis affect kids, about how to identify when children are having a difficult time, and about how to talk to them in ways that help. The following sections include some things we've learned about children in different age groups:

Taking Care of Little Ones

In general, younger children are less upset by community-level events unless they are directly affected. However, their parents' stress levels, distraction, and agitation can have profound effects upon them. The reaction of adults around them can also have a profound effect upon their interpretation of, and response to, the developing incident.

Preschoolers, kindergartners, and first-graders are most vulnerable to feelings of fear and insecurity. Normal routines and stability are helpful to them, as are creature comforts and the sense of being protected. What you say to your child matters less than that it is said in a calm manner. Children look to their parents' reactions to help them make sense of external events. Be honest, but take the child's level of understanding into account. Avoid abstract or confusing ideas, avoid addressing your own fears rather than those of your child, and keep it simple. Determine what the child is really asking for before attempting an answer.

Increased separation anxiety, clinging, and comfort-seeking behavior are normal, as is quiet, self-directed play or self-comforting behavior. Some behaviors among younger children are indicators that the child is particularly distressed. Going to sleep (if not normal for the child), "drifting off," refusal to eat, or disorientation is cause for concern, as is frantic, undirected agitation, unusual intensity and duration of crying, or loss of bladder or bowel control. Interpersonal frustration and conflict or difficulty interacting within the family is normal. Fighting, assaults, or general pandemonium is cause for concern, as is extreme passivity that makes family activity impossible.

Taking Care of School-Age Children

School-age kids have different sets of needs from their younger counterparts. Again, community-level events will have less effect upon younger elementary students, with the same exceptions as given above. Of greater concern are the impact of media accounts and the effects of rumors. Some elementary-age students can react negatively to a threat because they may be confused about the nature of the threat and how close it really is. Due to media and entertainment saturation, many kids' perceptions of the world are overly simplistic and overly dramatic. Additionally, both boys and girls are vulnerable to feelings of guilt and responsibility regarding crisis events, and these feelings are aggravated by the feats of superheroes in movies and on TV. Children from seven to twelve years of age suffer from all of the same fears as younger children, but judge themselves harshly for having these feelings.

Postcrisis reactions can interfere with schoolwork. This is a natural reaction that has its basis in the brain's readjustment to shock. Nevertheless, a child may be punished for malingering. Not only do children judge themselves harshly for failing to perform as well as their peers, teachers often do so as well. Finally, to add insult to injury, we as parents tend to join in. The answer? Encourage your child's teacher to back off from top-level demands during the recovery period, and support what your child *can* do. The name of the game is to avoid negative labeling of the child as a "behavior problem."

Certain signs of deeper distress may emerge among school-age children. Regressive behavior may occur, and distress may be expressed indirectly in age-inappropriate ways. Agitated behavior may predominate and can take the form of acting out against rules and routine. This can present problems among siblings and peers. Extreme individual behavior can be contagious. One child's agitated reactions can set off both agitation and withdrawal in the rest of the family.

Taking Care of Early Adolescents

Younger adolescents (ages twelve to fifteen) have a great need for affirmation from others their own age. They tend to be highly interpersonally reactive and are more prone to group contagion effects. Younger adolescents give far more weight to what parents say than they would ever admit. My own research has shown that fathers in particular can be very helpful by showing concern and listening closely to what their children are saying. While standards and limits are always important, they are especially important following a crisis. It is important to realize that if the distress of the moment is acute and if parents do not help young people to feel better, those young people will be prime targets for peers ready to show them simple solutions to avoid feeling bad. The risk of drug use, fighting, or sexual acting out is very high during times of crisis. A good message to impart to your kids to help prevent these and other potentially harmful behaviors is to reassure them that their reactions are "normal reactions of normal people to very abnormal situations." Remember that behind the façade of "coolness" there is often a child who is desperately seeking reassurance.

Taking Care of Older Adolescents

Older adolescents bear the same vulnerability to potentially harmful coping measures as younger adolescents; the stakes just get higher. Fighting with weapons, high-speed driving, involvement in the drug subculture, and sexual promiscuity present clear and present dangers. Older adolescents face other dangers as well. By age sixteen or seventeen young people are engaged in forming a sense of identity that keeps not only adults but also other young people at a distance. They see themselves as individuals whose task it is to form a life. Beset by crisis-related anxiety or depression, older adolescents are likely to make premature life changes, such as dropping out of school, joining the military, getting married, or other binding decisions for which they may be unprepared.

Parent support is important here, particularly in providing guidance in decision making, in reaffirming identity and value structures, and in helping the young person obtain additional support when appropriate. Talk to your adolescent about short-term problem solving and long-range planning. If it looks as if his or her plans are shifting too quickly and toward premature and binding life decisions, shift the discussion back to what is at the root of the planned change. Sometimes fears are driving the decisions. Try to find ways to help your child articulate and address those fears.

By the time a person reaches adolescence, he or she may have already endured repeated crises. These past difficulties can shape responses to a new incident. Thus, young people can be unpredictable. If their emotions are so overpowering as to be intolerable, they may act out in childish ways, such as drinking, arguing, or withdrawal.

Older adolescents can suffer from mixed impulses to follow parental directions one minute and to take control themselves the next. This can result in great confusion and family difficulty. Additionally, they may be under the influence of substances, or undergoing significant distress from sources unknown to parents, clergy, or school personnel. Combine your personal support and guidance with opportunities for young people to channel their energies toward controlling crisis-related damage or helping others. Encourage them to reach out to others through service or fund-raising projects, or by taking political action. Consider helping them to become involved in the real world, but through a controlled structure, such as an internship or learning program.

YOUR NOTES

_____

_____

_____

_____

_____

_____

_____

_____

_____

_____

_____

_____

_____

_____

What If You Suspect a Child Is Being Hurt or Abused?

As I said before, tension and uncertainty in the world "out there" or in the larger community can cause anxiety at home or in the school and make a local crisis more likely. Stress undermines coping skills, and people who normally keep control of their impulses may lose control when the situation is intense. Parents or teachers may easily become more angry and less careful in their treatment of children, as can police, doctors, and other professionals who work with them. Responsible adults must be vigilant regarding the well-being of children in their care.

> In the months following the 9/11 attacks, nine-year-old Gina Moore was acting more strangely than her parents expected. Although the entire family was jumpy, Gina seemed disproportionately affected. She began to "play sick" to avoid going to school, and then started ditching class to hang out at a classmate's home. She expressed reluctance to go to a parent-teacher conference. When questioned, she reported that the teacher had struck several other students and had verbally abused her. Her mother questioned other parents, and finally they confronted the principal. Their concerns corroborated other reports the principal had received, and the principal spoke to the teacher. Charges were filed and the teacher was removed from the classroom. Gina's disposition improved, as well as her attendance and performance.

In keeping an eye on your children's well-being, look for both *direct* and *indirect* signs that something may be amiss, as outlined below.

Direct Signs of Abuse or Victimization

There are four basic types of abuse, explained below with some of their direct signs:

EMOTIONAL ABUSE is when one person is emotionally or verbally assaulted by another person; there are no specific direct signs

NEGLECT/MALTREATMENT is a failure to provide for basic safety and needs; the direct signs are hunger, medical needs are unmet, clothing is shabby and neglected, the person or child is abandoned

PHYSICAL ABUSE includes batteringand injuring of a person or child by another; the direct signs are unexplained bruises, burns, fractures, or other injuries

SEXUAL ABUSE is when a person or child is forced or manipulated to ahve sex with another person or other pserons; the direct signs are difficulty walking or sitting, torn or stained underclothing, genital or anal bruises or bleeding, and venereal disease (especially in preteens)

Indirect Signs of Stress, Abuse, or Victimization

Often in cases of child abuse, direct signs are not present but certain changes in the child's behavior provide evidence that *something* is wrong. The cause *may* be a personal crisis or problem, or a delayed reaction to a community crisis. On the other hand, the behavioral changes can also be indirect signs of abuse. These indirect signs should be considered red flags, not evidence. If you see any of the following signs, talk over your observations with people you trust, including teachers, a mental-health professional, or police.

The signs below are broken down by age levels, but each level may include behavior from the previous level. In other words, elementary-school-age children often show preschool/kindergarten-age reactions mixed with reactions more appropriate to their age.

Among preschool or kindergarten-age children you may see . . .

Withdrawal. Children may become unusually quiet and seemingly detached from others. They may act subdued and possibly even become mute with adults or peers.

Denial. Denial may take many forms, including denial of facts and memories of events, avoidance of certain themes or issues in play or discussion, and ignoring certain people or conditions. (Note: Lack of conceptual understanding may be mistaken for denial.)

Thematic play. This encompasses frequent participation in reenactments or ritualistic play following a theme of either the trauma itself or life upsets that are secondary to the trauma (such as family problems or circumstantial changes).

Anxious attachment. This behavior includes greater separation anxiety and anxiety concerning strangers. Clinging, whining, refusing to let go of parents or favorite objects, and tantrums are frequently observed signs. Since such behavior often occurs during this developmental stage, look for changes in frequency, duration, and intensity.

Specific fears. Some common specific fears include fear of new situations, strangers, males, confinement, violence, or certain objects.

Regression. Under severe stress, children attempt to master the situation by reverting to behavior patterns they found successful at earlier developmental stages. This represents a search for a comfort zone.

Among school-age children you may see any of the above, plus...

Performance decline. A decline in performance in one or several areas may indicate a posttraumatic reaction among school-age children. School and intellectual performance, sports, music lessons, and other hobbies could all be affected.

Compensatory behavior. Behavior designed to compensate for the critical incident or its resulting loss, injury, or unwanted changes may be evident. Such behaviors may be attempts to deny, reverse, or gain retribution through fantasy, play, or interaction.

Obsessive talking. Once the child feels free to talk about the incident, he or she may talk about it continually. This is a necessary part of the process of assimilating the event and will likely be temporary.

Discrepancy in mood. The child may express feelings or moods that seem inappropriate to the immediate situation or to the events he or she is describing. Sometimes this represents an attempt to avoid full realization, and other times it is the result of the child's preoccupation with past events.

Behavior changes or problems. These may include getting into trouble, sudden changes in interest, or regressive behavior. Often these behaviors result from attempts to relieve anxiety, gain needed attention, or sort through new, troubling information about the world or the child him- or herself.

More elaborate enactments. Reenactments become progressively more sophisticated, although often no more satisfactory than during early childhood.

Psychosomatic complaints. Stomachaches, headaches, digestive upsets, etc., are often very real symptoms of psychological distress. Sometimes they are thinly disguised bids for extra time and attention. Such complaints are often indirect communications about other issues.

Among adolescents you may see any of the above behaviors, plus . . .

Acting-out behavior. Perhaps because of a combination of peer influence and a need not to defer to parental support, adolescents often act out their distress in ways that are ultimately self-destructive. These can include isolation, truancy, drug and alcohol abuse, sexual activity, violence, delinquency, running away, or suicidal expression or attempts.

Low self-esteem and self-criticism. Adolescents are quick to blame themselves and to condemn their own reactions to crisis situations. They often have fanciful expectations regarding their control over situations, and anything that goes wrong is interpreted as a blow to their sense of power and independence.

Acting too old, too fast. This behavior is often seen among poverty-stricken children who must compete in the streets with adults, and among child prodigies who must deal with adults constantly. Likewise, traumatized adolescents sometimes develop lifestyles several years in advance of their chronological age. This often results in unfortunate, lasting choices.

Displaced anger. Crisis often generates deep anger. Because you may be the safest person the adolescent confronts during the day, you may be the unwilling and undeserving recipient of anger that has no other place to go.

Preoccupation with self. Trauma, and the resulting inner processing that must be done to sort through the meaning of the incident, can intensify the adolescent's normal self-centeredness. Normal postcrisis concerns regarding issues of adequacy are often aggravated by the loss of control experienced during the crisis.

Speak Up

Whenever you suspect abuse, do not allow fear to prevent you from speaking up. Talk to your child about what you see. Ask questions until you are satisfied. Talk to your partner and share ideas. Talk to your child's teacher and principal. Talk to a counselor. Access resources in the library or online. If any doubt remains in your mind, talk to the police. Children who are abused need advocates; their parents are the most important advocates they have.

Taking Care of Yourself after a Crisis

As events move on, any crisis you face will become part of the fabric of your family and will shape its future. Remember, however, that your ability to help your family depends upon your own sense of well-being. It is critical—once the incident is over—to address your own needs. Help yourself heal by using the following strategies:

- Review the event with other adults who are supportive.

- Keep track of your feelings, thoughts, sleep, and imagery.

- Talk to others. Ask for their input about how things are going and what they think you need.

- Eat and sleep well, exercise moderately; don't overextend yourself.

- Work at putting the incident into a narrative or story by writing and telling others about it. (See "Things to Think and Write About" in the main text for questions that can guide you in doing this.)

- Find a creative expression for your feelings both at the time the crisis happens and later. Use activities like music, dance, and art to process deeply and express things you can't otherwise get out.

- Process the experience with a mental-health professional.

- Understand and accept your own need for acknowledgement and nurturing; look for that attention and support.

Your ability to be open to your family's needs and your responsiveness to them depend upon your own sense of well-being. By taking care of your own needs you can be strong for others.

Some Emergency Resources

The following resources provide helpful information about preparing for, responding to, and recovering from an emergency. Become familiar with these resources before an emergency happens; download or print out useful material ahead of time in case Internet access is impaired during the emergency.

Emergency Calls
Call 9-1-1. During a large-scale emergency you may not be able to reach 9-1-1 because the lines may be overloaded. If you can't get through, refer to the emergency-preparedness material available through the other resources listed below.

State and Local Resources
Look in the community-services section of your telephone directory for local resources.

Each state has an office of emergency services. Directions for how to contact your state's emergency agency can be found on the website of the Federal Emergency Management Agency's Global Emergency Management System:

www.fema.gov/gems/g_cats1.jsp?group1=102&groupName=
State+Emergency+Management+Agencies+%28U.S.A.%29

Each of the state emergency offices operates a website that provides regional information as well as contacts to local and county-level emergency services.

If the emergency is large-scale and located in your area, local radio stations will broadcast the locations of public relief shelters. Information about shelters can also be accessed through the local offices of the American Red Cross or Red Crescent.

Centers for Disease Control and Prevention (CDC)
Information specific to biological, radiological, and chemical threats can be found at the Centers for Disease Control and Prevention (CDC), which is part of the U.S. Department of Health and Human Services. This organization provides preparedness information, epidemiological updates, directions for emergency response, and links to other resources:

Phone: (404) 639-3311
Main website: www.bt.cdc.gov

Further, the CDC operates an emergency website titled "Whom to Contact in an Emergency":

www.bt.cdc.gov/emcontact/index.asp

The CDC also offers a website that provides contact information for state and local health departments as well as for a wide variety of other health- and emergency-related agencies and organizations:

www.cdc.gov/other.htm#states

Disaster Preparedness

Because phone lines and websites are likely to be overloaded in the event of emergency, it is a good idea to access and download important informa- tion beforehand. Critical information should be stored in hard copy.

The Federal Emergency Management Agency offers a website and a book for citizen preparedness:

Website: www.fema.gov/areyouready

Copies of the book, titled *Are You Ready? A Guide to Citizen Preparedness,* are available through the FEMA Publications warehouse at (800) 480-2520.

FEMA also operates a website for general disaster information, including preparedness, response, and recovery:

www.fema.gov/library/dizandemer.shtm

Practical information about what to do in the event of a biological, radio- logical, or chemical emergency is downloadable from the CDC websites listed above.

Mental Health

The National Institute of Mental Health offers a vast array of information about general mental-health needs and resources:

Phone: (301) 443-4513

Website: www.nimh.nih.gov/publicat/index.cfm

Information is also available at the following websites:

American Red Cross: www.redcross.org

International Committee of the Red Cross: www.icrc.org

International Federation of Red Cross and Red Crescent Socie- ties: www.ifrc.org

Children

The National Institute of Mental Health offers information specific to children's mental health:

Phone: (301) 443-4513

Website: www.nimh.nih.gov/healthinformation/childmenu.cfm

A general health website for children is sponsored by the Office of Disease Prevention and Health Promotion (part of the U.S. Department of Health and Human Services):

www.healthfinder.gov/kids

The International Society for Traumatic Stress Study sponsors a website listing trauma-related nonprofit organizations and foundations. Many of these provide information and materials to families about trauma:

www.istss.org/resources/nonprofits.htm

YOUR OWN EMERGENCY NOTES AND CONTACTS

Conclusion

The strategies and approaches in *Helping Your Family During a Crisis: An Emergency Guide* provide tools to deal with immediate reactions to crisis. Identifying reaction levels, using heads-up approaches to stabilize feelings and behavior, providing support and guidance—all of these lessen the crisis and increase our capacity to respond effectively. Understanding when and how to use these techniques enables you to become the center of calm in the middle of the storm, helping others to regain their own capacity for acting wisely.

Unfortunately, crisis events do not end their destruction when the fires are put out, the winds cease blowing, the injured are treated, or the dead buried. As much as we hunger for the hurt to go away and for things to return to normal, it takes much longer than we would like. Not only do we pay for the repair of buildings and lost objects, we also have much to do to repair our spirit and recover our peace of mind. Trauma is the gift that keeps on giving—memories and reminders can haunt us for months and years. Symptoms such as anxiety and depression, fear and disconnection, can undermine our efforts to regain the life we had. Until we put our internal life in order, the recovery process continues. . . .

After the Storm

Healing after Trauma, Tragedy and Terror

The second book in our volume provides a more comprehensive approach for understanding and dealing with the lasting effects of major crisis and life change. In it you will also find an important— and possibly unique—perspective: Much of our normal response to specific crisis is charged with deeper meaning because of social and global events that are unfolding around us. Understanding ourselves and our loved ones requires understanding this dimension.

It also helps to understand our reactions at a biological level, and to understand the way in which the mind attempts to make sense of disaster. With these perspectives in mind, the book then explores specific, practical approaches to healing the lasting hurt of crisis.

Contents

Part II: Tools for Hope and Healing

Acknowledgments

Over the last three years, this book became a larger and more comprehensive project than originally intended. Sometimes, however, as the path becomes steeper it also becomes more important, leading us beyond our anticipation into new and valuable territory.

Hunter House is a very special publishing company; they believe in their projects and insist upon working together to bring out the best writing possible. Acquisitions editor Jeanne Brondino and publisher Kiran Rana have provided fruitful feedback and solid inspiration the entire way. Developmental editor Kelley Blewster was a joy to work with and she and editor Elaine Ratner added greatly to the organization and detailing of the project. Thank you all for your outstanding and constructive support.

Many others provided significant and tangible assistance during development. While the book's shortcomings are all mine, I do little more than gather together the collective wisdom of those from whom I have learned. Some deserve special note. For sharing their award-winning insight, perspective, editorial eye, personal stories, and unflagging encouragement, I wish to convey my appreciation to Joanne Tortorici Luna, Victoria Bruner, Osborne Reager, Jim Swalberg, Norma Casas, and Elizabeth Sides. They each know the part they played.

As usual, I must admit and acknowledge the cost of the project to my family. I can't seem to avoid the long hours away, nor the preoccupation and frayed nerves I bring home. To Wendy, Trevor, and Whitney, once again I deeply appreciate your tolerance and forbearance.

A Note from the Author

As a trauma therapist and crisis consultant, I am afforded a rare inside view of life. I've worked in communities shaken by mass murder, terrorist attack, earthquakes, and myriad other overwhelming events that deconstruct ordinary lives and leave enduring marks. I've spent months—sometimes years—in my trauma practice helping good people reconstruct themselves and their lives after bad things have happened that shook them to their very roots.

Yet through all this, I have gradually become an optimist. I have watched people rebuild their lives in the aftermath of events that defy belief. Through my work I have been privileged to witness ordinary people like you and me learn to rework their circumstances and set off in new directions that offer new meaning. If you come to me with tales of trauma and calamity, I will patiently wait out your belief that all is lost. Things may be painful beyond description. Intolerable, perhaps; maybe even catastrophic. But is all lost? No.

While events of the past several years have brought challenges and confusion, they have also offered an occasion for personal growth and renewal. This inner journey requires new perspective and direction.

This book is about moving on. It provides maps to help you find ways to regain control and rekindle the joy of living. If you are struggling with insurmountable events and changes, if you are buffeted by reactions, thoughts, and feelings that defy control—then you are in the middle of a deep transition. As Winston Churchill once said, "If you are going through hell, keep moving!"

Introduction

On a cold morning in February of 2003, I sat with the school crisis team in Lower Manhattan. Nearly a year and a half had passed since the September 11, 2001, terrorist attack. In the difficult months since the attack this group had worked with traumatized staff and students, fighting a gallant fight against fear and despair, often overwhelmed by the scope of the event and the needs of the schools. The day before my visit the government had raised the terrorist warning level to a new high. There were suggestions that more planes might fly into buildings, bio-warfare agents might be released in the subways, or even a nuclear strike could occur. This team did not take such warnings lightly. They knew at a cellular level what chaos means.

Few people know the inside story of what happened in Lower Manhattan schools on 9/11. Six schools evacuated through blinding dust and falling debris. Courageous teachers and staff put aside fears for their own safety and that of their families in order to protect their students. Children dodged dead bodies and parts of bodies. Hours were spent waiting for parents who couldn't reach their children, not knowing for sure whether they would come at all. A sea of police, firefighters, emergency vehicles, and flashing lights—all were inadequate to set things right. The world had turned upside down before their eyes. Through this Dantésque scene—and the eighteen dreadful months that followed—the team persevered. They handled their own personal reactions and tended to the needs of their schools.

I was there that February morning to teach them new skills and provide them with tools for hope. I didn't want the meeting to digress into yet another dreadful recounting of their 9/11 stories or a stultifying description of the insurmountable obstacles they faced. However, we did have to acknowledge the intensity of the moment and the courage of the teachers and staff who braved the streets and subways to come in on this particularly frightening day.

I asked them to close their eyes and focus on their predominant emotion. I wasn't asking them to reveal it, I assured them, but only to report its intensity. Use the following one-to-ten scale, I suggested: If one equals no feeling at all, and ten equals overwhelming feeling so intense you can scarcely tolerate it and are about to shriek and run out of the room, where does your intensity level fall right now? We each called out a number.

The average emotional intensity level that day in that group was eight. These folks had been hammered so badly by circumstance and were so deeply affected by government reports of another imminent attack that they were ready to burst. Their intense feelings were triggered by the threat level and compounded by their personal experience.

Yet in a strange way, they were the lucky ones. They were fortunate because in the face of desperate challenge and daunting odds, and despite their own wounds, they had a mission. They were warriors in defense of their students. There were tangible actions they could take against the forces of chaos. Most of us don't feel we have that option.

Times of Uncertainty

Global events seem to be spinning out of control, affecting us deeply and creating a new backdrop for our lives. In the face of great uncertainty we each respond differently. Many of us cling to accepted truisms of the past like life rafts. Others question the motives and abilities of our government and power structure. Political and social divisions within our communities are widening.

The politics of terror uses fear to affect political change. It's working. Mounting economic, political, and social uncertainties rob us of our sense of well-being. An increasing number of people are beginning to question whether our material way of life is compatible with the rest of the world. We worry about our ability to stop antagonizing others, to defend ourselves, to establish order without sacrificing freedom.

Living in the New Age of Anxiety

In the late 1950s and early 1960s the world woke up to the possibility of nuclear annihilation. For the first time in history humankind could end itself within hours. Political brinksmanship had pushed weapons development to such an extreme that at any moment the end of the world could be upon us. Bomb shelters were dug. Schoolchildren were taught to hide under desks, as if that could provide safety. We had entered what writers at the time called the "Age of Anxiety."

Today a new age of anxiety is upon us. There is no army big enough, no array of nuclear weaponry or foreign policy aggressive enough, to protect us from one another. One individual with a satchel full of plastic explosive, biological contaminant, or any of a host of other portable weapons can bring down our lives. The second-largest terrorist strike in this country's history—the bombing of the Federal Building in Oklahoma City—was carried out by an American self-appointed patriot armed with a truckload of fertilizer. Like schoolchildren of the fifties crouching under our desks, we await whatever will happen next.

This new age of anxiety has a corrosive effect on the very structure that provides us the most stability. We want our homes to be our sanctuary from the tumult of the world. Our families should be the support system that we rely upon when all others break down. Yet faced with the gnawing uncertainty of the current world situation, the home fires sometimes turn into conflagrations.

We have to understand that this is a predictable by-product of the politics of terror. Fear eventually makes us angry, especially when it cannot be directed at the source of the threat. Chronic, low-level fear—anxiety—resulting from uncertainty and the constant threat of imminent chaos makes us very angry. Unfortunately, those we love are the ones most likely to walk into the path of our pent-up anger. Because our resilience and our tolerance for frustration are worn, because we are chemically wired to strike back, and because those we live with are in the same state of mind, we see our homes as vulnerable. They can become the arena where displaced anger is discharged.

Anxiety's Impact on the Family

A curious thing happened during the months following the September 11, 2001, terrorist strikes on New York and Washington, D.C. My private psychotherapy practice became unbalanced. For years my practice had consisted of three general types of clients: trauma victims, folks with family problems, and professionals (therapists, educators, and clergy). While the overall client numbers had varied somewhat, the proportion of each type—a third each—had been fairly consistent. After 9/11 the total number of clients shot up. But interestingly, the majority of the new clients were not direct survivors of the attacks; they were families—families in great turmoil.

They argued and fought bitterly. Old grievances had become intolerable. New offenses multiplied. Personal mannerisms became unbearable. Most importantly, these families were unable to avoid getting into arguments, and the arguments exploded into out-of-control fighting. Much of our time was spent creating rules of engagement: coming up with new strategies for limiting the intensity of conflicts, and finding exit strategies to avoid damage. It was as if anger were welling up like geysers from underground volcanic fire.

This phenomenon repeated itself when the government rapidly escalated the terrorist threat level in February 2003. Another surge of new clients arrived at my door. Again, most of them complained of family difficulty and most were fighting. Mine is just one practice; although the number of couples I saw was small, the implications were much bigger. The pervasive fear that gripped the world was undermining these relationships.

Personal Crisis Against the Backdrop of Fear

Did you ever wonder why so many love stories in books or films are set during times of war? Or why many stories of self-discovery or coming of age are told within the context of disaster or at times of historical change? A colorful milieu lends immediacy and drama to everyday events. Drama begets drama. Personal events gain energy from their context. Personal crises become more serious, more poignant, and more significant when they play out against larger ones.

This means that the new age of anxiety adds fuel to the normal problems of living. It lowers our resistance to stress and places greater demands on our personal resources. We—and those we love—are more vulnerable now to the immediate effects of crisis and the erosion of despair. More than ever before we need tools to deal with crisis on a personal level.

No one gets through this life untouched by personal crisis. In one of my early studies I found that middle-class children, who in general had led fairly sheltered lives, had suffered an average of at least one event that could be classified as traumatic by the time they were seventeen. Even when we are held transfixed by distressing world events, personal crisis and drama may strike.

How to Use This Book

I'm wondering what brought you to this book. My guess—given the times in which we live and the book's title—is that you are dealing with the aftereffects of a significant shake-up in your life. Like geese flying in a storm, you may feel as if you have been blown far off course.

I have gathered together the best insights, strategies, and approaches I know to help you pick up the pieces and move on. Here you will find stories you can relate to, explanations you can understand, and techniques you can use. This is more than a book about coping, however. Each chapter invites reflection. Most contain a section titled "Things to Think and Write About," which encourages you to explore how the concepts presented in the chapter relate to your personal experience. In this way, you can seek the deeper meaning of your experiences and explore who you are and where you are going.

A special Emergency Guide is located at the front of the book, to give you quick access to the information you need most when you are preparing for, coping with, and recovering from a crisis. It includes step-by-step guidelines for action, tools for recognizing and dealing with stress reactions, and even questions to ask yourself to help you take control of the situation. There is a focus throughout the Guide on providing support to children—from little ones through older adolescents—including specific suggestions for talking with them and drawing out their feelings. Much of the information in the Emergency Guide is presented in greater detail and with fuller explanations in the main text, which follows. An appendix at the end of the Emergency Guide contains contact information for federal, state, and local emergency agencies.

Part I of the main text reviews the personal side of global uncertainty. World events, such as terror strikes, war, political hysteria, economic shifts, and rapid change, combine to create stress on an individual level and within families and communities. Within this distressing context, we may also be faced with personal loss and tragedy that subsequently take on added meaning. Here you are encouraged to assess the ways in which stress manifests for you personally. This section gives you the basic facts necessary to understand your reactions to overwhelming personal and global events. Stories and commentary describe the body's emergency response, how the brain functions during normal times and during emergencies, the need for the mind to integrate crisis experiences, and the effects of delayed and complex reactions to traumatic events. It sets the foundation for planning how to manage the distress that follows chaos.

Chapter 1 summarizes the reactions to uncertainty and fear many people are now reporting.

Chapter 2 takes a closer look at such reaction clusters as fear and anxiety, disconnection and withdrawal, and exhaustion and depression.

Chapter 3 focuses on the body's natural response to crisis, and how our basic survival instincts can go awry, causing acute stress.

After the crisis has passed, memories of it shape our worldview. Chapter 4 examines how this process works as well as the specific effects of "hot" and "cold" memories.

Looking further into the future, Chapter 5 explains the signs of delayed reactions to trauma that can occur months or even years after the event, and demystifies the extreme case of posttraumatic stress disorder.

Chapter 6 focuses on complex trauma, wherein past traumatic experiences add to the effects of new ones.

Spirit and attitude, the keys to spiritual balance and recovery after trauma, are discussed in Chapter 7, which looks at the higher-order human need for purpose, effectiveness, connection, and integrity.

Part II provides specific tools for handling personal crisis and taking care of yourself afterward. Chapter 8, in particular, contains essential information: ways to recognize your overwhelming reactions and bring them back to normal. It provides concrete strategies for managing fear and panic, anger and rage, and overwhelming loss. Other chapters offer a comprehensive approach for stabilizing family emergency and longer-term personal reactions.

Chapter 9 explains how you can recover from reactions of anger, fear, and debilitating sadness.

Chapter 10 focuses on coping with withdrawal, depression, and dissociation, and explores the consequences of attachments to the past.

Caring for our families is of utmost importance after a traumatic event. Chapter 11 is a guide to stabilizing your family, especially your children, and for dealing with family arguments.

Perhaps you or your family would benefit from professional help. The role of professional therapy is explored in Chapter 12, which offers explanations of several types of therapy as well as advice on how to choose a therapist and ways to best use a therapist's help.

When you've handled your short- and long-term reactions to crisis, the final challenge is reconnecting with your loved ones. Chapter 13 provides insights and useful tips.

Chapter 14 is about personal spiritual practice and how it can benefit you, whether or not you are a religious person.

And finally, the concluding chapter attempts to put the various situations we all find ourselves in into perspective, especially emphasizing the stabilizing power of our connections to our communities and to each other.

Global Uncertainty and the New Age of Anxiety

CHAPTER 1

Living in Troubled Times

Just after 9/11/2001, someone famously stated that "Everything had changed." What's changed now, a number of years later? Or, perhaps we should ask, what hasn't changed?

During World War II, GIs had a favorite word: SNAFU. It meant situation normal, all fouled up. It expressed the feeling that confusion, complications, and incompetence were normal and expected. In everyday life, not just the military, things usually do not go as smoothly as we would like. On the other hand, things seem to be particularly difficult nowadays. The GIs had another expression for times that go beyond the expected foul-ups, times when things are so bad we can hardly make sense of them. It was FUBAR: fouled up beyond all recognition. In some ways, the times we are going through seem to have moved from SNAFU to FUBAR. We can hardly recognize the world or remember how things used to be just a few years ago.

Sources of Uncertainty

Several years after the events of 9/11, how many people, even as far away as the West Coast, are still bothered by their reactions to that fateful day? According to one of the first long-term studies of the aftermath of the terrorist attacks, a great many folks are still shaken and are awaiting new attacks. Psychologist Suzanne Thompson, of Pomona College in Southern California, interviewed over five hundred people, none of whom even knew anyone in the attacks. Even after correcting for concern over the ongoing war in Iraq, Thompson found that fully 60 percent of the people she talked to expressed levels of fear and anxiety higher than they'd felt before the attacks. Many were afraid to fly in airplanes, were not reassured by increased security measures, and believed that they were vulnerable to another attack. Nearly 20 percent said they suffer ongoing reactions that are the same as they experienced immediately following the attack. For a great many Americans, the effects of 9/11 are not dissipating and, in fact, are more widespread than most recognize.

Hurricane Katrina stands as an example of one of the many events that have occurred since 9/11/01 that continue to aggravate our sense of personal vulnerability and social confusion. Katrina came as one of a set of unusually serious storms that many scientists link to overall global warming. Its initial fury was compounded by the breaching of levees protecting downtown New Orleans. The Federal Emergency Management Agency, led by a political appointee with no disaster experience, moved slowly to respond. This compounded the effects of the disaster upon the efforts of the already overwhelmed local governmental agencies. Charges of incompetence and cronyism were further complicated by allegations of favoritism and racism. All of this was capped off by the noncompetitive awarding of millions of dollars in recovery contracts to friends of the administration for cleanup. The point here is not to blame officials for the mishandling of the incident. If only it were that simple! Rather, the real lesson to make clear is why the individual dramas lived out among the thousands of suddenly homeless and displaced survivors are so poignant to the larger society. Events never take place in a vacuum, even events that seem out of control. Victimization occurs in a context. Even those who were not directly affected watch on. If it can happen to others, they reason, it could happen to me. The effects of Hurricane Katrina further undermine our belief that we are protected by our social structures.

Living in Fear: The Effects upon Our Health

When we live in constant dread of further catastrophe, our health is affected. Fear, uncertainty, and loss create stress. Yet the specific ways in which we are affected are often confusing, both to us and to the professionals who try to help us. Symptoms pile upon symptoms in ways we have difficulty understanding. Old diagnostic categories sometimes just don't fit.

Suppose you have been experiencing shortness of breath, difficulty sleeping, obsessive thoughts about new terrorist attacks, fears about the future, problems relating to your family, loss of interest in your job—and you figure the whole world is going down the toilet. A doctor tells you that you are suffering from stress and ought to slow down. (Not so easy to do when you have to pay your mortgage, hold down your job, or put your kids through school.) Another doctor tells you that you are suffering from anxiety. She gives you antianxiety medication. It doesn't help. So you go to a third doctor who says you are depressed and prescribes an antidepressant. Meanwhile, your spouse is insisting you meet with a family therapist. How can these people draw such different conclusions from the same symptoms? More to the point, what do you do when things are unbearable, but none of the normal categories or cures seems to fit?

Is It Stress or Trauma?

The concept of stress first emerged as a corporate issue in the 1970s. In that context, stress was seen as the chronic activation of the body's fight-or-flight reaction in response to work-related demands, such as performance pressure, too many hours, difficult working conditions, etc. In the 1980s and 1990s the use of the term *stress* was generalized to describe people's reactions to an assortment of fairly common events, such as life-threatening disease, family difficulties, and addictions. Seen in this light, the reactions many of us have to the unwinding of our way of life seem to be much more than a case of stress.

Our reactions also seem to be more than general anxiety. Fear reactions abound, with good reason. On both an individual and a collective level, we respond to reminders of our situation in one moment by experiencing agitation and intense reactions, and in the next moment by sliding into numbness and withdrawal. To me this looks more like traumatic stress than it does mere anxiety.

Indeed, the concept of traumatic stress provides a helpful perspective on our contemporary malaise. During the 1980s the media popularized the notion of psychological trauma as a stress reaction to extreme events. Trauma was initially described as a reaction suffered by some veterans of the Vietnam War. Then it came to be seen as a reaction to a single-incident, high-intensity event, such as a devastating automobile accident or a personal assault. Finally, the term *trauma* was extended to encompass reactions to ongoing (chronic) experiences like incest, child abuse, or domestic violence. Trauma resulting from such events is a classic, clinical reaction to extreme experiences.

VIVIAN'S STORY

Vivian Jackson works as a hairstylist in an upscale salon in a Chicago suburb. She has two children in elementary school and a husband from whom she separated four years ago because he had physically abused her. Vivian works hard to pay the bills, be a good mom, and still have time for friends. The divorce is pending despite the fact that both of them want it. Vivian can't face a court appearance, and the mere thought of finally being free from Bob—no matter how difficult their life together was—sends Vivian back to her therapist.

The morning of 9/11 just about sent her back to Bob. She was on her way to work when her mother called on the cell phone and told her to turn on the news. Not only had New York been hit, it was thought that the Sears Tower in Chicago was the next target. Vivian immediately headed back to school to pick up her children. The next several hours were a nightmare. If her mom hadn't come over, Bob would have, and Vivian would have let him.

Since then Vivian has experienced anxiety attacks and has fought to maintain her sense of direction. She has watched her community change, her financial situation grow precarious, her children's school deteriorate, and her country go off to a war she doesn't understand. She has frequent headaches, she feels numb and disconnected, and things simply don't make sense to her anymore. Most of all, she fears for her children. She lives on constant alert for signs of further terrorist activity. Vivian is putting on weight (a proven reaction to chronic stress) and losing interest in things that used to excite her. She scans the headlines every morning but then quickly turns to the comics section. She doesn't trust politicians and avoids talking about world events with others because doing so just makes her mad. Vivian often quotes a friend who is only partly joking when she says, "Depression is anger without enthusiasm."

Vivian is not alone. According to the professional literature, websites, the news media, and reports from individuals in therapy, a great many people are reporting

- constant anticipation of impending disaster
- a preoccupation with televised news

- flashbacks and replays of terrorist strikes
- intense anger and irritability at home or on the road, often misdirected at others
- pessimism about the future
- nostalgia or flights into sentimentality
- fear for loved ones and their futures
- alternating between overprotective parenting and feeling that nothing really helps
- problems sleeping, nightmares, and strange dreams
- chronic anxiety and depression
- specific fears
- vague but pervasive feelings that something is deeply wrong
- changes in behavior and lifestyle
- a philosophy of "live for today and let tomorrow take care of itself"
- feelings of futility
- questioning of personal values and directions
- weight loss or gain
- a compulsive desire for comfort food or familiar rituals
- a desire to be rescued
- marital and relational difficulty
- exhaustion
- desperation
- a sense that everything can change in a minute, that nothing is permanent

Many of these reactions look like traumatic stress. Certainly, reactions of fear, anticipation, and anger resemble trauma, particularly if they alternate with feeling disconnected, exhausted, and depressed.

Contemporary Angst and Personal Crisis

About a hundred years ago, European writers coined a term that seems more fitting now than it did then. *Angst* refers to the dread and anguish we feel when we realize that things around us are spinning out of our control, but that we must act anyway. Sociologists used the term to describe how ordinary citizens felt as they watched their old ways of life destroyed by the powerful forces of impersonal industrialization. Now we feel a similar sense of loss, disconnection, and vulnerability. Political, economic, and technological forces beyond our influence increasingly shape our world. We feel powerless to protect our families—and ourselves—in any meaningful way.

This is the context, then, in which unfolding events mix with past experiences, contemporary angst, and everyday crises to produce the blend of symptoms we struggle to understand. It is our job to survive—and to survive meaningfully. To do so, our task is to sort through our reactions, learn how they are formed, and find ways to address them.

CHAPTER 2

Your
Personal Response
to Tragedy, Terror,
and Uncertainty

The world is more confusing and frightening than ever. And we are certainly more confused and frightened. We go through our days acting as if everything is all right but waiting anxiously for the next turn of events that could throw our lives even further off balance. The "new normal" we hear about doesn't feel normal at all. We ponder the absurdity of things like government announcements that the threat level has been raised to "very high" and that we are to simply go about our business as usual with a "heightened sense of awareness." Times like these can make a person crazy!

Life is never really easy. It continually brings challenges—during the best of times and these not-the-best of times. Regardless of the state of the world, people get sick, lose jobs, get into accidents, and have family problems. We get overwhelmed, anxious, or depressed. We have midlife crises. All of these trials of living play out against the backdrop of the times in which they occur, and are colored by them. Sometimes it is hard to discern whether individual reactions—anxiety or depression, for example—are the result of larger community events or are simply made worse by them. It can be very confusing.

If we seek to address the issues in our lives that we don't like, we must begin by gaining clarity about just what is going on. This chapter invites you to take a serious look at the specific ways in which you are being affected by the events in your life, large or small, whatever their origins.

Nothing Occurs in a Vacuum

Whatever trials we face within our own souls, these trials are shaped by circumstance. Whether we struggle with anxiety, panic, failure of nerve, or temptation to drink or behave badly, our personal drama plays out on a particular stage. To understand our trials we must first place them within their context. If you think about it, it makes sense that global, national, and community events have had an impact on your life. You have probably felt some changes in your family, neighborhood, and workplace since the 9/11 attacks, and these changes have probably had an effect on you. But people react to different things. Which particular changes are key to understanding you and your responses?

Your Personal Sense of Well-Being

Political challengers often ask voters, "Are you better off now than you were four years ago?" Such questions press home the issue of overall well-being. *Well-being* is a blanket term that covers your sense of security, comfort, and general happiness. While everybody's sense of well-being has been affected by the events of the past several years, specifically *how you* are affected depends upon your individual situation. Consider the following cases of Bob Searles and Maria Chavez:

> *Prior to 9/11, Bob ran a small-parts distribution business. His clients were larger companies that provided the myriad parts needed in aircraft assembly. In the aftermath of 9/11, aircraft production slowed, as did the demand for Bob's parts. By the fall of 2002, his business had just about bottomed out, and so had Bob. On a one-to-ten scale measuring well-being, with ten being the highest sense of well-being, Bob's feelings hovered at around two. He was depressed, suffered from low self-esteem, and was pessimistic about his future. He felt inadequate to continue what he was doing and too old to try something new. By the fall of 2003, however, aircraft production had begun to climb again. Job orders were trickling in, and Bob's efforts to develop interests beyond his business were paying off as well. His sense of well-being began showing signs of recovery.*
>
> *The events of 9/11—while distressing—initially had a lesser impact upon Maria. A teacher in California, Maria had always felt a*

deep sense of mission that, if anything, was strengthened after the attacks. During the fall of 2002, Maria's sense of well-being was at least a seven on the same ten-point scale. But when California was battered by energy and financial scandals, and the political mael-strom that followed, the state's educational spending plummeted. Programs were cut back severely. Suddenly Maria had about 50 percent more students in her classes, many of whom were facing a bleak future. Soon after, Maria was notified that she was being moved into an inner-city school marked by violence, where she was asked to teach subjects for which she was poorly prepared. By the fall of 2003, she was losing both her sense of mission and her sense of well-being.

Both Bob and Maria were profoundly affected by events far be-yond their control. They reacted differently because the 9/11 attacks affected their daily lives differently. As the level of stress in their work situations changed, both experienced shifts in their sense of well-being.

Consider where you stand right now. Do you feel—in general—that things are okay? Are you reasonably comfortable, and do you feel fairly secure? Do you feel good about yourself and optimistic about the future? Has your level of well-being changed over the past few years?

Filling out the graph on page 61 will help you compare your sense of well-being prior to 9/11—or Hurricane Katrina or any other milestone crisis in your recent past—with how you feel now. You can either write directly on the page or draw a similar graph on a separate piece of paper. Make a mark on each vertical line indicating how you felt or feel most of the time, with 1 representing the lowest sense of well-being and 10 repre-senting the highest. Connecting the marks will show how your sense of well-being has changed.

Getting Down to Specifics

Changes taking place at the community and global level that affect our general sense of well-being manifest themselves in specific reactions. Gen-eral stress can wear down our bodies and our relationships. We can be dis-heartened by too many demands and by a belief that our efforts don't matter. This wear and tear results in specific reactions that may occur in the following clusters:

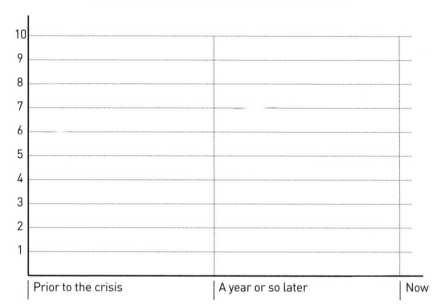

CHANGES IN YOUR LEVEL OF WELL-BEING

- Confusion and disorientation
- Fear and anxiety
- Irritability, anger, and difficulty getting along with others
- Disconnection and withdrawal
- Exhaustion and depression
- Physical problems
- Changes in behavior

Whether your world was suddenly turned upside down or gradually became more difficult, you may be experiencing a number of these reactions. The following sets of questions will help you explore the ways in which your thinking, feelings, relationships, health, attitudes, and belief systems have changed. Consider writing down your answers to the questions that speak to you. The purpose of these exercises is to find a pattern of reaction that can then guide your personal approach to self-care and renewal.

Confusion and Disorientation

Do you notice that you can't think as quickly as you used to? Do you find yourself unable to react as efficiently? Have your beliefs and assumptions about safety and well-being changed? How about your theories of how things work and of what's right and what's wrong?

Think about the ways in which your thinking and beliefs have changed, and about how these changes have been demonstrated in your recent behavior. Which of the following are you experiencing? (Check them off in the following Confusion and Disorientation Inventory Chart, or write them down on a separate piece of paper or in a journal.)

___ Difficulty making sense of even small things

___ Trouble prioritizing

___ Constant confusion over why things are the way they are

___ Difficulty remembering how things used to be

___ A desire to be rescued by someone stronger

___ Vague but pervasive feelings that something is deeply wrong

___ A philosophy that says, "Live for today and let tomorrow take care of itself"

___ Questioning of your personal values and direction in life

___ Other, similar reactions (list them)

_____

_____

You might wish to write about or draw something that depicts how these reactions are affecting your life.

Fear and Anxiety

Are you growing more anxious or fearful? Do you fear losing your job, or having it become more difficult or more dangerous? Are you concerned about the future of your children or the next generation? Do you worry about acts of violence in your community or new acts of terrorism?

Sometimes we know exactly what we are afraid of. At other times our fear doesn't have a specific object; we are anxious about things in general.

Which of the following are you experiencing? (Check them off in the following Fear and Anxiety Inventory Chart, or write them down on a separate piece of paper or in a journal.)

___ Constant anticipation of impending disaster

___ Preoccupation with televised news

___ Flashbacks and replays of terrorist strikes

___ Feelings that everything can change in a minute and that nothing is permanent

___ Fear for loved ones and their future

___ Problems sleeping, nightmares, or strange dreams

___ Episodes of panic

___ Other, similar reactions (list them)

_____

_____

Write about or draw something that depicts how these reactions are affecting your life.

Irritability, Anger, and Difficulty Getting Along

Are stress reactions robbing you of your ability to tolerate frustration and to work well with others? Do you feel like you want to strike back at whoever is threatening your well-being and the safety of your loved ones? Sometimes fear and anger express themselves indirectly—bursting out of us before we can stop them, often attacking people who don't deserve it, such as counter clerks, other drivers, coworkers, or people we love. Which of the following are you experiencing? (Check them off in the following inventory chart, or write them on a separate piece of paper or in a journal.)

___ Intense anger and irritability at home

___ Conflicts and drama at work

___ Road rage

___ Yelling at clerks, shopkeepers, or others

___ Trouble getting along with family or friends

___ Anger at yourself

___ Anger toward certain groups of people

___ Blame or misdirected anger

___ A strong desire to take disproportionate or unrealistic political action

___ Other, similar reactions (list them)

_____

_____

Be specific about any reactions or patterns you are becoming aware of.

Disconnection and Withdrawal

Sometimes our work, our personal lives, or the world is just too much to bear. If you are having difficulty, and others around you are too, it can be hard to get along or to get things done. Do the pressure and changes in your daily routines feel intolerable? Do you simply want to escape? Do you find yourself shutting out the world?

Shutdown can take the form of disconnection or withdrawal. We feel we just can't face another person or another demand on our dwindling energy and time. We want to take care of our own hurt and retreat from what Sartre called the "hell of other people." But each time we make the choice to withdraw inward, we cut off one of the things that make us human: our sustaining relationships. Indicate any of the following that apply to you:

___ Feelings of futility

___ Pessimism about the future

___ Retreat into solitary activities

___ Avoiding real connection with coworkers and colleagues

___ Avoiding people you know and places where you might meet them

___ Feelings that things are "surreal" or dreamlike

___ A loss of feeling

___ Giving up goals or dreams

___ Getting lost in "if only" thinking

___ Other, similar reactions (list them)

_____

_____

Consider writing about the ways in which any of these signs of stress are affecting your work and relationships.

Exhaustion and Depression

Are you running on empty? Coping is a lot of work. It takes energy to live with fear and uncertainty and to handle all the things that can and do go wrong. Our bodies and minds can perform in difficult circumstances for a long time, but eventually they need a break. Exhaustion and depression can set in and rob us of vital energy. Depletion can take a variety of forms, including withdrawal, burnout, loss of interest, and fatigue. Do any of the following characterize you?

___ Feelings of depletion

___ Feeling easily overwhelmed by others or by negative thoughts

___ Physical and mental exhaustion, or chronic fatigue

___ Frequent low-level depression

___ Occasional bouts of serious depression

___ Feelings of desperation

___ Preoccupation with loss

___ Constant rumination about matters

___ Feelings that it just isn't worth the struggle anymore

___ Other, similar reactions (list them)

_____

_____

Do your specific reactions impede your life and sense of well-being? Sometimes signs of exhaustion simply signal a need to get more rest, relaxation, and enjoyment. At other times, they can represent a serious mental or physical imbalance. Depression or dissociation can be very serious and even life-threatening. See a mental-health professional if these signs have become troubling, or if other people point them out to you. It may be difficult to bring yourself to admit the severity of your fatigue, but you have everything to gain from professional assistance.

Physical Problems

Is your body telling you something? Fear, anxiety, anger, or other intense feelings can manifest in symptoms resembling physical illness. Our stomachs may hurt or we may have headaches—arising not from illness, but from more general distress. This can be particularly true for those of us who tend to discount and minimize our feelings and attempt to carry on in the face of hardship. The complicated chemistry of stress can result in wear and tear on our most important body parts. The following physical signs have been associated with distress. Indicate any of the following that apply to you:

___ Stomachaches

___ Loss of appetite or eating binges

___ Weight loss or gain

___ Aches and pains

___ Shortness of breath

___ Heart palpitations

___ Headaches or tension in neck, shoulders, or back

___ Frequent illness; inability to snap back from illness

___ Skin irritations or other skin conditions

___ Other, similar reactions (list them)

_____

_____

Any of these may be signs of chronic stress or low-level trauma. On the other hand, they may signify serious physical diseases. If you write them off as stress, you may be ignoring a dangerous illness that can be treated. Whenever you have physical signs of distress like these, your first stop should be a doctor's office. If you get a clean bill of health, you can consider your physical ailment a possible result of distress and deal with the upset directly. Write or draw about any patterns you see or reactions you are having.

Changes in Behavior

Are you doing things that you did not normally do in the past? Are you seeking comfort in the familiar, returning to old patterns of behavior— whether they were healthy or not?

As we struggle to cope with the changes in our world, those of us who are recovering from addictive or compulsive disorders are at risk of relapse. The rest of us are at risk of becoming involved with what seem to be easy answers to a challenging situation. In the name of coping, we are likely to dig ourselves into a deeper hole. Which, if any, of the following are you experiencing?

___ A compulsive desire for comfort foods or familiar rituals

___ Nostalgia or flights into sentimentality

___ Sudden changes in behavior and lifestyle

___ Alternating between overprotective and apathetic parenting

___ Taking more risks than usual

___ Alternating between compulsive spending and hoarding

___ Overuse of alcohol or other substances

___ Relapse into addictive or compulsive behaviors

___ Obsessing over certain thoughts or details

___ Working far too many hours when it isn't really necessary

___ Other, similar reactions (list them)

_____

_____

You may want to write or draw something about your specific behavioral reactions.

Attitudes and Beliefs

So far we have explored the basic reactions to difficult experiences and changes in our world. We can call these "stress signs" or "symptoms of distress." Some of them are more serious than others, and each person has his own particular mix of reactions. In addition to distress symptoms, you may be experiencing reactions on another level entirely. Ongoing fear, uncertainty, and symptoms of distress can erode your underlying views of the world and of your life. Such shifts in attitudes and beliefs can reduce your spiritual energy in the following four areas:

- Sense of purpose and meaning
- Belief that your efforts are worthwhile and effective
- Feelings of connection with others, a higher power, or your deeper self
- Conviction that your actions are consistent with who you are and the values you hold

If your attitudes and beliefs have shifted in any of these ways, you are not alone. In later chapters we will discuss specific attitudes and beliefs that are linked to overwhelming stress and will consider ways to work at renewing your spiritual energy.

THINGS TO THINK AND WRITE ABOUT

1. How does it feel to look at the inventory charts you filled out in this chapter, particularly in light of world events?

2. What do your entries suggest about you and your life?

3. When you look at your comments, do you see any implications for your future?

4. Do the inventory charts help you see more clearly how others around you are responding to global and local events as of late?

5. Does writing about your reactions to the recent changes in the world help to clarify your perspective?

CHAPTER 3

How Our Body and Brain React when We're Threatened

We all want to be able to cope during difficult times. The simple truth, however, is that sometimes we fall apart. Sometimes we respond to life-threatening or emergency situations by acting badly. And sometimes we find ourselves reenacting a difficult situation long afterward.

In the face of terror or tragedy, your greatest tool is the one that brings stabilization and resilience to you and your family. Whether you are coping with an incident within your home or one that is community-wide, your first line of defense is to create the calm that allows you to take constructive action. If you can bring peace to yourself, you can spread it to others around you. When the real enemy is chaos, the best tools for hope are those that help you manage fear, anger, panic, and despair.

Some events are more likely to overwhelm you than are others. They may be hard to cope with because of their intensity, the grotesque nature of the sights and sounds, or the threat they pose to your well-being. They may be overwhelming because they remind you of other serious incidents, because they hold special meaning for you, or because they are symbolic of larger circumstances. Your reactions are caused not just by the events themselves, but also by what you bring to the situation.

In addition, you should consider the following:

- Some events may be overwhelming for others, but not for you.

- Some events may be overwhelming for you, but not for others.

- Some events may be overwhelming for you one day, but not the next.

- Some complicated situations may overwhelm you over time.

Some Helpful Terms

Language can be confusing, and the words we use to describe our stressful experiences can actually make things either better or worse. The following are some definitions to help keep our discussion clear:

Incident: An event causing a stress reaction.

Crisis: A situation that we perceive as placing us in jeopardy. Our reactions to crisis may be severe, sometimes delayed, and sometimes ongoing.

Stress: The psychological and physical reaction of an individual to a distressing or traumatic incident.

Burnout: A state of emotional exhaustion caused by constant exposure to unwelcome change, threat, and problematic personal reactions.

"Angst": A twenty-first-century version of the "angst" described by writers during the Industrial Revolution. It combines elements of dread and foreboding with feelings of emptiness and dislocation.

Traumatic stress: Leftover reactions (lasting emotional scars) from overwhelming events. "Traumatic" because these reactions originated in extreme experiences, and "stress" because they continue to plague the lives of those traumatized.

Complex trauma: Stress caused by multiple traumas or by traumatic events that took place over a prolonged period. Trauma symptoms can "layer up," so that the pattern of reactions to a recent situation can reflect several past events in ways that are perplexing.

Acute stress: Extreme reaction to an incident, usually taking the form of overreaction (panic, rage, or loss of control) or underreaction (shutting down of feeling and/or thinking).

How We Respond to Crisis

To better manage your reactions, it will help to understand how people generally respond to abnormal and extreme situations. Our success as a species has always depended upon a quick response to emergency conditions. Imagine two Neolithic Age adolescents walking down to the watering hole in the early morning. A tiger jumps out of the bushes and charges toward them. Terrified, one of the boys runs away without even thinking. The other thinks for a moment about how best to handle the situation. Which one of the boys will be breakfast for the tiger, and which will go on to contribute his DNA to the gene pool?

The human body is hardwired for survival. In order to respond quickly to emergencies, it has to be able to override reflection. While conscious thought is essential to solving complicated problems, it is a hindrance to immediate action. Thus, in our evolution, we have developed two sets of response patterns—one for normal times and one for emergencies. During nonemergencies, our nervous system directs blood flow to digestion, opens up our higher brain centers for reflective and abstract thought, and lowers our heart rate, respiration, and blood pressure. The body is set for sustained concentration and constant energy flow. We can call this the *parasympathetic nervous system*, or the *relaxation response*.

During a crisis, however, our bodies shift almost instantly to survival mode. Blood is redirected to major muscle groups. Our heart, respiratory, and blood-pressure rates increase. Emotions directly drive our thinking and responding. We can call this the *sympathetic nervous system*, or the *fight-or-flight response*.

The fight-or-flight emergency response allows us to quickly

- prepare our body for survival reactions
- focus only on survival-relevant factors
- use emotions to drive actions
- ignore ruminations and irrelevant and distracting thoughts and feelings
- feel pain less acutely
- access only crisis-related memories

Stress Triggers a Chemical Cascade Inside Us

Marie Sinclair, 83, was grandmother to eighteen-year-old Billy Sanderson. Billy liked to work on his 1959 Volkswagen at his grandmother's house because it was easy to park it at the bottom of the sloped driveway. The side-mounted jack wasn't quite tall enough to allow Billy to crawl under the car to work unless he could angle the car just so. Grandma's driveway was perfect for that. Although she didn't like Billy's being under the car, Marie did enjoy having him around and was baking cookies while he worked.

Marie heard a loud noise from the driveway and looked out. The jack was lying on its side, and Billy's legs were protruding from under the car, jerking spasmodically. He was pinned and couldn't breathe. Marie did not panic or become enraged or hysterical. Rather she rushed to the car, squatted down by the front bumper, and lifted it off of Billy. Marie was in physical therapy for nearly a year repairing her cut and bruised fingers, torn ligaments, sprained muscles, and dislocated vertebrae and ribs, but Billy lived.

How could Marie Sinclair do this? How was she—barely 107 pounds soaking wet and eighty-three years old—able to summon the tremendous strength necessary to lift a heavy car? How was she able to concentrate on what had to be done and not fall apart under pressure? When asked later how she did it, Marie had no answer.

Her body did, however. When faced with life-threatening emergencies, the body responds with an immediate cascade of chemicals that activate the fight-or-flight response. Three sets of chemicals worked together to produce the response that saved Billy. We can call the first set *arousers*. These chemicals allow the body to rapidly accelerate its response to a crisis. They supercharge the nervous system, sparking an energy release that translates immediately into action. At the same time, awareness is sharpened, the brain focuses on the cause of the threat, and memory banks of threat-related recollections are opened for automatic reference. The body launches itself either toward the threat or away from it.

This reaction can quickly spiral out of control, however. The body can become agitated to the point of ineffectiveness, the mind can become fixated, and the emotions can race out of control. To prevent this, the body releases a second set of chemicals we can call *moderators*. These have the effect of reining in the arousal reaction. They prevent the panic, rage, or hysteria that would thwart effective action. The body is allowed to access arousal energy without losing control, so the emergency reaction can be used to address the threat.

The third set of chemicals focuses the body's energy. They explain Marie's ability to ignore pain and attend to the task at hand. For convenience, we can call them *blockers*. They allow the body to direct its emergency reactions without being slowed by concerns unrelated to the crisis. This third group of chemicals—similar to opium and morphine—flooded through Marie's body, providing a temporary analgesia, which allowed her to push herself beyond pain. She literally did not feel the cuts, tears, and snapping in the tissues of her hands and arms. It also shut down her emotional reactions and gave her a feeling of euphoria so that she looked beyond the distress of the moment. It provided a "tunnel vision" that allowed her to do what needed to be done.

Feeling little emotion or pain, and seeing only what had to be done, Marie was able to spring into an action that saved her grandson and surprised everyone. This is truly a survival system. When in balance, this chemical cascade allows the body to take maximum action in order to meet perceived threats. When it's out of balance, however, things work out differently.

When Things Fall Apart: Acute Stress

Officer Linda Martinez responded to an early morning blaze in a residential neighborhood. As she pulled up, flames were already coming out of the house's windows and neighbors were gathering. When the fire engines arrived, Linda helped to establish a perimeter to keep people back. As far as she knew, all the family members were out of the house and were gathering across the street. The fire broke through the roof, and soon the entire house was engulfed. It was a bad situation, but so far everyone was under control. Suddenly, a car careened up. "Mija! My baby!" screamed the driver, emerging from the car. The woman, apparently an aunt, ran directly toward the house. Overcome by her rising distress—irrational and agitated— the woman threw herself past the crowd in an apparent effort to run into the inferno. It would have cost her life. Linda had to forcibly restrain the woman to prevent further injury.

Police officers or paramedics have learned to expect the unexpected from people at the scene of emergencies. Victims are impacted not only physically, but also psychologically. Crisis situations are inherently chaotic, and sometimes the onlookers react chaotically. No one expects the victims of a crisis to act normally. But emergency workers have found that witnesses and passersby often have reactions similar to those of the victims, and their responses often become part of the crisis.

Overreaction and Agitation

How and why do some people fall apart in emergencies? We have observed the *how:* When the fight-or-flight system malfunctions, people either explode into extreme emotional action or collapse into psychological shock. Both of these responses qualify as acute stress responses. Knowing how the body's marvelous emergency system works can help us respond to crises. It can also help us understand how things can go wrong. Driving the acute stress response is an imbalance of the arousal, moderating, and blocking chemicals in the brain. That imbalance is what underlies the *why.* Understanding how this work gives us the key to managing our reactions.

If, during the fight-or-flight response, insufficient moderating or focusing chemicals are released, the body becomes overaroused. The surge of adrenaline (an arouser) released into the system creates spectacular effects that spin out of control. Thoughts race, memories of previous crises flood the mind, pulse and heart rate peak, and the body becomes agitated. The ability to prioritize actions, think rationally, and control behavior is lost. Emotions drive behavior: Fear shifts to panic; sadness becomes hysteria; anger turns to rage. The predominant emotion at the time becomes the only emotion.

An overreaction or agitated response includes the following features:

- A flushed appearance
- Irrational thoughts
- Emotional extremes
- Agitated behavior

Agitation presents an obvious problem during a crisis. Behavior is disturbed, coping becomes impossible, and the threat is not addressed. Paradoxically, the agitated person feels as if the situation is overwhelmingly threatening and everyone else is unaware of its gravity. The more others attempt to calm him, the more alarmed he becomes. Overreaction can result in actual danger, because judgment is impaired and impulses can become uncontrolled.

Fading and Shutdown

Although "losing it," or overreacting, is the more obvious form of acute stress response, it is the less common one. The other, more common, reaction is underarousal. When insufficient arousal is combined with an overflow of the third set of chemicals, the blockers, the person goes into psychological shock. This can take the form of "shutting down" or developing tunnel vision; of becoming anesthetized and too disconnected to act or becoming overly focused on partial details and unable to see the whole incident or picture. In short, she "fades" in the face of overwhelming stress. Others may fail to immediately notice this behavior because the person becomes so quiet. People suffering from psychological shock often sit in the background, out of the way. Sometimes they stand around with blank looks on their faces. In extreme cases, they may become nearly immobile and dazed.

A faded ASR (acute stress response) includes the following features:

- A pale, vacant appearance
- Confused thinking
- Flat emotions
- Slowed behavior

In a situation that represents an actual threat, an underreactive person cannot mobilize his or her defenses. Confusion precludes action. The world appears to be spinning; other people seem to be racing about in disarray. Nothing makes sense, and more importantly, nothing seems to matter.

It is important to know that the faded form of acute stress response occurs twice as often as the agitated form. This means that many people are psychologically wounded without anyone being aware of it. You may have experienced this reaction without you or others realizing it. It is even more important to know that shutdown is a stronger indicator of future negative reactions (delayed symptoms) than overreaction.

Being able to recognize acute stress reactions can help us identify those most in need of support during crisis and those most at risk of developing symptoms later. It can also help us to understand our own delayed stress reactions, which can arise even if we feel we were not impacted at the time of an incident. For more information about acute stress response, see Chapter 9, which explores the response in more detail and offers techniques for managing it.

Any experience of tragedy, trauma, or terror can be complicated and confusing. I hope this brief discussion will help you begin to sort through and make sense of your experience. The following chapters will examine the body's emergency response to crisis in more detail, including taking a deeper look at how the brain functions during an emergency, and how the brain records memories of crisis events in a way that creates delayed stress reactions. Understanding these connections will help you stabilize your reactions and craft a solid self-care approach.

Chronic Fear and Anxiety Can Create Episodes of Acute Stress

Chronic, low-level fear and anxiety can also touch off episodes of acute stress response. Anxiety is different from emergency-based (normal) fear. Normal fear is prompted by clear and present danger. It triggers a release of the hormones that activate the mind and body to respond efficiently. Chronic fear and anxiety follow different prompting and neural mechanics. They are longer lasting and more general than normal fear, and they keep the body in a constant state of arousal. The brain is constantly bathed in stress-related hormones—lower levels than those created by fear, but continuous. Both brain and body are negatively affected by the constant exposure to adrenaline, cortisol, and other emergency hormones.

If you suffer chronic fear and anxiety, your memory can become impaired and your immunity to disease can be weakened. You can develop high blood pressure and stomach ulcers. Further, those parts of your brain that override the emergency response, by evaluating threats and putting them into perspective, can be weakened by constant exposure to emergency-based brain chemicals. This can change the way you interpret experience, magnifying the effects of bad news. You may see threats where they do not exist, see them as more threatening than you might otherwise see them, and, as a result, you may overreact. This condition can also affect your ability to tolerate frustration, delay gratification, and get along with others. Your learning can be affected, and your ability to perform on the job or in the classroom can deteriorate.

When you are constantly on guard, you easily blow things out of proportion. Relatively minor incidents can trigger full-blown acute stress responses. These episodes of acute stress reaction can undermine your life. Gaining control of chronic fear and anxiety reactions as well as emergency responses is central to the fight for stability.

THINGS TO THINK AND WRITE ABOUT

- If you've ever lived through a serious emergency, what happened? Was it one event or a series of events?

- Is there a history or context that gives the event special meaning to you?

- How did you react at the time?

- Is there a difference between what you felt at the time and the way others describe the situation?

- Have you ever considered writing a personal account of how things in your life changed as a result of what happened?

CHAPTER 4

Seeing the World
Differently after Crisis
and Trauma

A baby crawls across the carpet. Its eyes and ears are wide open—and so is its mouth! To its parent's consternation, anything the baby can lift goes into its mouth, and its mouth goes around everything else. It seeks to know and to grow. Although the human brain has some genetically determined structure, much of it is pliable; it changes to meet the demands of experience. As the baby crawls across all of the carpets life puts before it, the baby's mind seeks to absorb everything—all of life's new experiences, whether good or bad.

This drive to learn from experience never stops. As the tabloid proclaims, "Inquiring Minds Want to Know!" Watching, listening, and wondering, we take in the world. We absorb a vast array of facts, and we assemble from those facts a picture of what to expect from the world and from ourselves. We seek knowledge as a means of avoiding risk and making our lives safe.

When bad things happen, we take note. Our brain records these events in a way that helps us avoid similar pitfalls in the future. This chapter explores the special way the mind learns from trouble, and the way that learning shapes our future for better or for worse. Understanding how this process works will help you in your efforts to deal with reactions to crisis that have become troublesome.

Building a Worldview

Imagine yourself at one end of a billiard table. You strike the white ball with a cue stick, sending it crashing into the cluster of colored balls and scattering them across the table. The game can stand as a metaphor for the world as we know it. It plays out in terms of

- action/reaction
- cause and effect
- beginning/middle/end
- predictability
- preferred outcome
- natural laws
- imposed rules

As in a game of billiards, no single event shapes the world. People and places stand in relationship to one another. Events unfold in sequence, and one thing leads to another. We make sense of seemingly random events by seeing the interconnections and relationships behind them. When we are able to figure out how things work, when we come to understand the connections among things, actions, and events, we are happy. Our understanding allows us to predict events, anticipate dangers, avoid pitfalls, and take action to get what we need. It is about survival. We are programmed to seek meaning, because meaning keeps us alive.

The Outer "World" as an Internal Construction

When a baby is discovering the world by mouth, touch, and hearing, it weaves the sensations it experiences into ideas about the objects it encounters. Those ideas are stored for future reference. All new sensations are understood by referring to the stored memories. In this sense, reality is not just "out there," it is also in our heads. This doesn't mean it is a fantasy or that it isn't real. The inner world we construct is a map. It steers our journey and provides a guide by which we make sense of what philosopher David Hume called the "buzzing, bursting confusion" of our sense experience. More precisely, our inner world is the experience we have of our outer sensations. Without it our sensations would be pure chaos.

Memory is the process of storing past experience and using it to understand present events. Understanding how things work is essential to predicting the future. This involves perceiving what happens, relating it to prior experience, and projecting an outcome. The baby, having discovered that furry animals sometimes bite, may begin to avoid them. The ability to sense "probable outcomes" gives us the key to taking effective action. Memory is critical to this process. Memory allows us to create, maintain, and use our map of the world. The philosopher George Santayana once said, "Those who are ignorant of history are doomed to repeat it." We can make an even stronger statement: Those who are ignorant of history are likely to be blindsided by the future.

You Are What You Remember

Memory gives us a sense of time, identity, and continuity. In part factually accurate but always interpretive, memory builds maps of our experience, using a vast storehouse of previous experiences for reference. Through this library of information and interpretation, we can make sense of present experiences and plan for what might happen next. Memory construction is a work-in-progress. As demonstrated daily in courts of law, memories are not set in concrete. They are malleable and undergo constant revision. Lawyers cross-examine eyewitnesses to review testimony in order to determine how much is accurate and verifiable and how much is tainted by personal interests or beliefs. The courtroom comedy film *My Cousin Vinny* dramatically demonstrates the subjectivity of memory. A novice lawyer, portrayed by Joe Pesci, brings in witnesses one by one to revisit and reconsider their memories of what they thought they saw. Each comes to realize that what they believed happened was unsupported by the facts and that their conclusions were premature.

<u>Crisis, Memory, and Survival</u>

The mind is not a camera—and for a very good reason. The brain needs to do more with memory than put together a photo album. It needs to classify and sort the incoming information economically, because it encounters an overwhelming amount of information each day. Much is repeat news. Some is novel but irrelevant; a little is novel and important. Once in a while, a new experience arrives that makes us revise an existing interpretation.

The mind uses memory to construct its internal map, and it does so in a way that is adaptable to new information. This can be a problem when a crisis occurs. A crisis demands the quick absorption of information. When the brain, using incoming visual data, identifies a creature it recognizes from previous experience as "tiger," it needs to send a message to the body saying, "Run!"

How does the brain determine what information is normal "world-view" material and what is immediately critical to survival? How does it know when to think things over and when to jump? To solve this dilemma, the brain has developed two different kinds of memory; we will call these "cold" and "hot" memory.

Cold Memory

Normal, nonemergency processing of memories entails sorting and integrating new information into the internal map. This higher-order mental process is generally ongoing and seamless. While some pieces of information take longer than others to assimilate, most fit immediately into existing logical orders. This process of learning proceeds rapidly from childhood through early adulthood. The brain itself is relatively plastic during this time; it develops its size and configuration partly as a result of the specific experiences it encounters.

Sights, sounds, and touches are normally taken in, mixed with thoughts, feelings, and reflections, and combined into a sensible order. The order is set in time; memories are organized into beginning, middle, and ending sequences. The various parts of experience, including sensory bits, emotional reactions, and logical connections, are related to one another. The results are transferred up to the higher centers for storage and further processing. This is what the brain of the baby, who is forever crawling around exploring its world, is up to.

The key to cold memory is repetition. When we learned our multiplication tables, most of us managed the task through repeated exposure to the various combinations of math facts: 1 x 2 = 2; 2 x 2 = 4; etc. When we learned how to get along with others, it was through trial and error. Experiences become associated over time, as neural pathways are laid down by repeated activation.

Our mental map shifts and expands as we learn and grow. We fit new experiences into our existing repertoire of classifications and concepts, expectations and predictions. Our decision making becomes streamlined through habit and continuity. How could it be any other way? Imagine waking up every morning and deciding whether or not to get up, or what side of the bed to get upon. Imagine stumbling into the bathroom and weighing the pros and cons of shaving first and then using deodorant. Or vice versa? Or maybe not cleaning one's body at all? Our personal sets of mental, emotional, value-based, and intentional expectations simplify and strengthen our ability to focus upon longer-range issues. The existence of habits and routines makes life possible.

But what happens when the unexpected happens?

Hot Memory

Besides everyday "cold" memory, the human brain has evolved another kind of memory, one dedicated to remembering emergency information. It has direct connections to the autonomic nervous system (the part of the nervous system that governs involuntary processes, such as secretion of hormones and digestion). When called into action, it takes priority over our normal memory system. We can call memories stored in the emergency system "hot" memories.

I know a woman who cannot drive on freeways because she suffers flashbacks related to a terrible accident she had several years ago while driving on a freeway. The accident almost killed her and her unborn baby. Her memories of the accident are hot memories; they are connected closely to her brain's emergency center. To this day, certain situations, such as approaching a freeway on-ramp, cause her emergency memories to surface quickly. This, in turn, triggers great fear and panic. These delayed reactions (so called because they occur long after the initial traumatic event) make getting on the freeway impossible for her.

This postcrisis interplay of hot memory and delayed reaction to a traumatic incident is further illustrated by the following story:

> *Troubled by an unexplainable incident from the previous day, Betty Thompson sought counsel from her good friend Mindy over coffee. She explained how she had been delivering a legal document to an office on the eighth floor of a building downtown. Everything was fine until she entered the building and found her way to the elevator. Suddenly, when the elevator bell sounded and the door opened, she became dizzy. The hallway seemed to spin, and she couldn't get her breath. Betty tried to force herself to enter the elevator but couldn't. She fled the building and ended up paying a delivery service to take*

*the document to its intended destination. Since then, Betty had been
confused and shaken.*

*Concerned, Mindy asked, "Do you remember anything unusual
when you entered the building lobby? Was there anything strange
about the elevator or anybody in it?"*

*Betty shook her head. "No, in fact, I don't go downtown very often
since...."*

"Your rape last fall?" Mindy probed gently.

*Betty looked up intently. "You know what? Yesterday was the first
time I've been near an elevator since then. That's where I first
noticed that guy."*

"In that building?"

*"No. In an elevator! The bell sounded, the door opened, and there
he was, staring at me."*

*Betty hadn't yet drawn the association between elevators and the
terrible, life-threatening experience she'd endured. Her body did,
however, the next time she tried to step into an elevator. When the
door opened, a special memory from the past alerted her emergency
response system that it was time to escape. Her overwhelming reactions made it impossible to remain. Betty was out of the building
long before realizing why.*

We have all lived through emergencies. Even in modern, civilized
society, we face occasional danger. When we survive near-hits, our conscious mind wants us to dust ourselves off and keep on living. Meanwhile,
our brains create a special database for survival. We record emergency
events for future reference, just as Betty did.

Flashbulbs in the Dark

Why do our bodies often react viscerally to hot memories, like Betty's did
when she lost her breath and felt the room spinning? Recall from Chapter
3 that under threatening conditions our bodies are flooded with emergency chemicals. This hormonal response to crisis—what we've labeled a
"chemical cascade"—creates an altered environment for memory storage.
These hot memory traces, laid down during crisis, are more indelible. And
they have more emotional content than cold memories. Sounds, images,
tactile sensations, and kinesthetic impressions are strongly associated with
the emotional reactions of the moment. These sensory impressions are

sometimes referred to as "flashbulb memories," because they freeze the scene in our minds.

Imagine entering a darkened room with a camera. It is too dark to see much, so you move around the room aiming the camera and shooting pictures. Every time you shoot a picture, the flash lights up the room momentarily. The brief image is captured on film and in your mind. The pictures you take may connect with one another or may not connect at all. When your body has an emergency response to a crisis, it stores memories like these flashbulb images.

Hot memories are also accessed differently than cold memories. This is because they serve a survival function. Whether or not they are processed and integrated into your worldview, they are intimately connected with your emergency response system. This keeps you ready to respond immediately when faced with similar situations. When you remember cold memories, you consciously recall the event in its fullness. When you remember hot memories, you may only see the flashbulb picture or have the same physical or emotional response. Like Betty faced with the elevator, you may not understand why you panic or fade away. Even memories you don't remember well can trigger acute stress response.

THE DIFFERENCES BETWEEN "COLD" AND "HOT" MEMORIES	
Cold memories	*Hot memories*
Normal intensity	"Flashbulb" intensity
Beginnings/middles/endings	Nonsequential
Sensory associations	Sensory fragments
Normal emotional range	Intense emotion or no emotion
Make sense	Sense doesn't matter
Rare physical associations	Marked physical associations

Cerebral "Indigestion" and Hidden Memories

What accounts for the hidden memories that seem to pop up out of nowhere, like those Betty experienced when she approached an elevator months after she'd been raped? During an emergency the brain is busy. It does not have time to do the elaborate higher-order processing of troubling, traumatic images and sensory impressions (the very things that eventually will turn into hot memories). They are boxed and shelved to be dealt with later. Sometimes, however, when memories are intolerable, the process can be interrupted. Memory images that are too intense—too terrifying or too rage provoking or too challenging to our worldview or our self-concept—may remain unprocessed. Both Betty and my friend who suffered the freeway accident experienced massive delayed reactions without clear awareness as to why they occurred. In simple terms, their memories of their respective emergencies were so loaded with intolerable emotion that they could not be integrated properly.

When this happens, we suffer a sort of emotional and cerebral "indigestion." The troubling memories are not forgotten, just ignored. They are stored in an incomplete form, just as they were originally experienced. They lie in wait, so to speak. They can fulfill their survival function without becoming objects of consciousness. The mind has a drive toward wholeness, however. It keeps trying to assimilate exiled memories. These memories can arise in the form of intrusive, distressing images: dreams, unbidden memory fragments, flashbacks, even body or emotional memories that are disconnected and troubling. They are the psychological foundation for the confusing mix of postcrisis reactions.

What It All Means

Hot memories trigger extreme responses that are sometimes the same responses—agitation or fading—that occurred during the actual moment of the incident. These responses can be momentary or lasting. They can be manageable, or they can reach the intensity of acute stress response as described in the previous chapter. The link between hot memory and stress reaction explains how the reaction to an emergency can persist long after the incident is over. Until the link is broken, a reminder of the incident will continue to trigger the response. Once the link weakens, however, the reaction will lessen. Although the memory will always have the potential to arouse a stress reaction, with successful treatment, the reaction can be managed.

As we have seen, the mind's preoccupation with making sense of emergencies and weaving emergency memories into the larger view of self and world has a troubling side effect: It can't let go of the past. Tragedy, terror, and uncertainty can create a firestorm of difficulties for us. To understand the true nature of our response to troubling times, we must explore delayed reactions and psychological trauma. This is the task of Chapter 5.

THINGS TO THINK AND WRITE ABOUT

- Think again about the traumatic event(s) you wrote about at the end of the previous chapter. Do some memories of it still trouble you?

- Do some of the memories feel "hotter" than others—that is, more vivid and fragmentary?

- Do reminders of the incident trigger the return of these memories?

- When these memories come, are they accompanied by feelings similar to those you experienced at the time of the incident?

CHAPTER 5

Is It Trauma?
Delayed Stress
Reactions

No matter how bad things get, we all need to cope. Even after dramatic, life-changing events, we get up the next morning, put on the best face we can muster, and head out to make the best of things. And for the most part we manage! We tuck in our troubles and pull our lives back together. For the *most* part....

Once in a while we aren't so lucky, and we carry an incident with us in the form of psychological aftershocks. Sometimes full-blown reactions do not surface for years after an event. After the crisis, adjustment seems to progress in a satisfactory manner. We may not have forgotten the incident, but it certainly seems to be behind us. Then—usually in the face of some sort of major life stress—trouble flares up. For days, months, or even years we look at the world and ourselves differently, sometimes overreacting to things, sometimes failing to handle situations well. People may remark that we seem different. Once in a while we may experience an acute stress reaction that we didn't anticipate and can't even understand.

Sometimes people have what are called *delayed stress reactions* to single incidents or troubling circumstances. These are reactions that are triggered by current stress but that are shaped by prior events. A delayed stress reaction may be fairly minor, it may be more serious, or it may even reach clinical proportions. This chapter explores delayed stress reactions in all of their varying intensity levels and suggests where in the book you can find strategies for coping. The purpose of this discussion is to help you make sense of the ways in which the consequences of challenging life events can play out over an extended period of time. Having this knowledge can help you to regain your peace of mind.

The Past Catches Up

During and immediately following difficult events we may suffer temporary psychological reactions. For the most part, we are usually successful in finding ways to cope with our reactions. We deal with disrupted sleep patterns; we follow old habits by showing up to work and meeting our family commitments. We shake off emotional upsets and occasional distressing memories. Often we are so successful at coping, in fact, that even *we* are convinced there was no lasting damage done. We may go for years without experiencing undue difficulty from postcrisis symptoms.

Yet life is full of surprises. In the process of living we periodically endure times of difficulty. Marital strain, job changes, losses, even normal stages of growth can test our strength and endurance. Sometimes, in fact, periods of normal life stress can exhaust the systems we've built for coping. During these times, delayed stress reactions may arise. We develop symptoms related to events we may not even remember. Mike Geffin's experiences bear this out:

> *Normally Mike Geffin had it all together. Mike and his brother owned a specialized church-furniture manufacturing company. Mike was the one who would meet with ministers or church committees and work out disagreements or deal with new demands that arose during construction. He prided himself on his integrity and his ability to work productively with diverse groups of people in stressful situations. Lately, however, he wasn't doing so well.*
>
> *Mike's brother, Tim, had called him in to talk about business concerns twice in the past two weeks. Tim reported that he had received several complaints from customers regarding their treatment at Mike's hands. They mentioned Mike's irritability and explosive behavior. One moment he would encourage their feedback, but the next moment he would grow hot under the collar, replying sarcastically or sometimes even getting angry and storming off the job site. The customers expressed concern that their needs were not being met as promised and that they had no recourse through Mike. Mike's response to his brother's queries was to go out and wash the company truck.*
>
> *There was trouble at home as well. Mike wasn't sure which came first, the stress at work or the conflict at home. Whatever the cause,*

home was no longer a sanctuary. It had become the battlefield. Mike's wife seemed chronically angry and ready to fight. Their sex life had become a thing of the past, and each blamed the other. Mike was spending more and more time going for drives in the desert in his four-wheel-drive pickup.

Something that happened during one of his drives got him in enough trouble to compel him to see a counselor. Seeking therapy had never been Mike's style, but this time he was badly shaken. Returning to the main road following a side trip, Mike had brought his truck skidding to a stop where the road dipped before rejoining the highway. A jeep was stopped at the bottom of the dip. Mike watched it carefully, gently releasing his door latch. Something about the jeep bothered him. He found himself sliding off the seat, pulling out his thirty-thirty rifle, and drawing down on the other driver, who was getting out of the jeep. Fortunately, he was able to stop himself in time. His actions surprised him nearly as much as they did the other driver. This wasn't the first time he had done something like that lately.

"And you don't have any idea why you did that?" asked the counselor.

"No, sir."

The counselor thought for a moment, then asked, "Mike, was there ever a time when your split-second impulsive actions saved your life?" Mike thought for a moment and then nodded.

"When was that?" prodded the counselor.

"In Vietnam. Lots of times."

"Tell me about one of those times."

Mike began slowly. "Okay…well, there was one time my squad was crossing a rice paddy. We were walking single file over the dike. It was quiet, but the birds were singing and no dogs were barking. A few Vietnamese were working the paddy. There was absolutely no reason to worry any more than at any other time. All of a sudden I panicked."

"What did you do?"

"I screamed, 'Fall back!' and we all ran back and took cover behind a lateral dike. The guys had come to trust my instincts. A set of mortar explosions started walking up the trail, right where we'd been. It was an ambush."

"What did you do then?" the counselor asked.

"My guys returned fire into the tree line, but I just looked up at the sky and asked myself over and over, 'What was it?' I had to figure it out, to know what to look for next time."

"What did you figure out?" persisted the counselor.

"I finally remembered that I'd seen one of the villagers lift her hand out of the paddy water to grab another bunch of rice plants. She had on fingernail polish. You just don't work all day in paddy water with fingernail polish on. She didn't belong there."

"Ah. And that's why you hit the panic button. You noticed something out of place, and it caused your massive reaction. And that's how you had learned to save your life and the lives of your squad."

"Yeah."

"And now you're under a lot of stress again," the counselor pointed out. "Your old ways of survival are surfacing again. But the reflexes that kept you alive then aren't working now. In fact, they are about to get you into a real jam."

Under serious but essentially normal life stress, Mike was showing behavioral symptoms of a delayed reaction to previous trauma. Wartime reactions from years ago were now emerging as delayed symptoms. His old reflexive behavior patterns had been deeply imbedded under combat conditions. They'd been buried when he'd resumed civilian life, to allow him to adjust to that life. Now that he was going through rough times, however, his earlier instinctual behavioral patterns began to resurface. Perhaps he was going through a normal stage of adult development. Maybe his marital difficulties felt overwhelming. In any case, his posttrauma behavior, related to combat, was now becoming much more of a problem than the current stress factors. His inability to handle interpersonal conflicts at work and at home was about to cost him both his marriage and his job.

Delayed stress reactions can be disheartening. Just when we think our lives are in order and our past forgotten, they drag us back to places where we don't want to be. Sometimes we don't even recognize our current reaction patterns as a delayed response to an old stress. It often takes a professional to see the connection between past and present.

Delayed Reactions to the Storms of Living

Intense feelings and behaviors that take place at the time of an event may reoccur when the mind revisits the event. Sometimes the reactions to a crisis continue in its aftermath, but in other cases the reaction lies dormant and then arises later under conditions of stress or some reminder of the crisis. Delayed reactions vary widely and can present a confusing picture. They can include

- unwanted memories that intrude into consciousness
- distracting thoughts about the event
- flashbacks (visual, auditory, olfactory, tactile, kinesthetic, or emotional reexperiencing of the event)
- distressing dreams and nightmares
- distress at exposure to reminders of the incident
- difficulty recalling or thinking about the incident
- depression
- loss of interest in things that used to be important
- feeling detached from others
- loss of strong emotions or numbness
- problems sleeping
- unreasonable anger or sadness
- trouble concentrating
- jumpiness
- substance abuse or problems controlling behavior
- difficulty with relationships

It's a long list! Sometimes things get worse before they get better. You may have experienced this in your own life. I know a Vietnam veteran who for fifteen years after he "returned" didn't realize his life difficulties were related to combat. It took him a long time to connect the things that were going wrong in the present day with what had occurred in his past. Once he understood the connection, however, he was in a better position to take constructive action.

The hauntings that plague us long after tragedies occur can go on and on. Furthermore, major life disruptions can have an additive effect. Like a snowball gaining size and momentum as it rolls down a hill, postcrisis reactions can take on a life of their own.

Sometimes the delayed reactions listed above are "subclinical"—that is, they don't qualify for diagnosis. If they do not impair your functioning and do not cause you distress or detract from the fullness of your life, they are simply part of the fabric of living. On the other hand, if they do impair functioning, create distress, or interfere with your living, they may be part of a larger cluster of symptoms and may qualify for a diagnosis such as anxiety, depression, behavioral disorder, or a number of other conditions that have standard treatment approaches.

Occasionally, the configuration of symptoms falls into a specific pattern called *posttraumatic stress disorder* (PTSD). There are several forms of PTSD, and they warrant further investigation here. Maybe you have PTSD and maybe not; either way, there is much to learn about the effects of tragedy, terror, and troubled times by understanding how trauma works.

Posttraumatic Stress Disorder: What It Is and Is Not

For years, people who suffered from PTSD were misunderstood. They were labeled moody, irritable, obnoxious, self-centered, crazy, and sometimes lazy. They did not fit the diagnostic labels of the time, but they were certainly suffering. In 1980, the American Psychiatric Association (APA) officially introduced the term *posttraumatic stress disorder*. The association set the guidelines for diagnosis in its handbook *Diagnostic and Statistical Manual of the American Psychiatric Association (DSM)*, which is currently in its fourth edition. While the concept has evolved somewhat since 1980, its inclusion in the *DSM* as an official diagnosis has helped thousands of people make sense of what initially appeared to them—and to those who loved them—to be a cluster of unrelated symptoms.

Perhaps you have been diagnosed as suffering from PTSD, or perhaps you wonder if you fit the diagnosis. PTSD is a complicated condition. This section sorts out the various components of PTSD as set forth in the *DSM-IV*. The material presented in earlier chapters will help you make sense of the components. First, though, we must begin by pointing out what PTSD is not.

What PTSD Isn't: Similar Conditions

PTSD is not the only condition that can develop following extreme experiences. Anxious, phobic, depressive, and dissociative reactions often occur following traumatic events. Sometimes they are serious enough to be clinically diagnosable, and sometimes they are not. Each of these types of reactions can make up part of the clinical picture of PTSD, but none qualifies on its own. They must occur together to be considered PTSD. Howard Li thought he had PTSD, but he learned that his anxiety disorder did not meet the criteria for PTSD diagnosis:

> *Howard Li taught physics at the local community college. For years he had been nervous about little things. He obsessed about upcoming events, overprepared for his lectures, and got upset when other colleagues dismissed his concerns as being frivolous. At home he was accused of overprotecting his daughter and spending too much time worrying about family finances. He had become increasingly vocal about his concerns over the past several months, and his obsessions were beginning to affect his work. A trusted friend and colleague took Howard aside and pointed this out. He suggested that Howard seek professional assistance in dealing with his anxiety. Because the friend knew that Howard had served in the Army during the Gulf War, he ventured the opinion that Howard might be suffering PTSD reactions to combat. Howard wasn't so sure. He did accept the idea that professional guidance might be in order, however. He couldn't dismiss the fact that everyone from his department head to his daughter seemed to be saying the same things about him. He scheduled an appointment with a local therapist who was known for his work with veterans. After several visits the therapist diagnosed Howard as suffering from anxiety disorder, and they discussed treatment options. Howard mentioned his colleague's concerns about the possibility him having PTSD. The therapist replied that Howard's anxiety disorder may well have stemmed from combat experiences, but it did not qualify as PTSD because he didn't have withdrawal or dissociative reactions. "Don't worry," he pointed out. "You've got your plate full dealing with the anxiety."*

Fears and anxiety, depression, or even dissociation are important clinically, whether or not they fit the pattern of PTSD. They can occur following serious events—that is, as a posttrauma reaction. Or they can develop without any reason you can identify. If you experience any of these symptoms seriously enough that they interfere with your life, consider consulting a mental-health professional to help you understand and manage your feelings.

What PTSD Is: Its Components

The American Psychiatric Association agrees on several conditions, or symptoms, that are necessary for a diagnosis of PTSD. The conditions must be present together, and the APA is very specific as to what constitutes each condition. This is because the defining characteristic of PTSD is the *interplay* among the various symptoms. To assist you in understanding the diagnostic criteria, and to help you decide if they fit your situation, this section lists and describes each of them.

Please note: This chapter is not intended to substitute for official diagnosis by a qualified clinician. It is included for informational purposes only. If you suffer from any or all of the following symptoms severely enough that your life is disrupted, please seek the help of a qualified mental-health professional.

The traumatic event must be seen as life threatening and overwhelming.

> *Bill Charlton was a first-year firefighter with the U.S. Forest Service. Within months of being hired, Bill's engine was assigned to protect a group of cabins from an approaching fire. The firefighters were quickly overwhelmed in a narrow canyon by a wall of flame and could not escape. They had to take refuge in their engine. For twenty-four minutes the fire washed over the engine. They relied upon breathing apparatus to survive, while propane tanks close to them boiled and threatened to explode. The noise was intense, as were the heat and smoke inside the engine. Without any chance of escape, Bill was terrified and had to fight panic.*

Key points:

- The event must be overwhelming.
- It must be perceived as threatening death or serious injury.
- It may be either firsthand experience or the witnessing of another's death, injury, or threat of such.

- The person must experience fear, helplessness, and/or horror.

The person must reexperience the event through haunting thoughts, preoccupation with the event, nightmares, fragmentary memories, or even flashbacks.

Monica had been held at knifepoint and raped repeatedly for hours in her car. Three years and much therapy later, she became romantically involved with a very nice man. On the drive home from a movie, they became involved in an argument stemming from the movie. He pulled over so the heated discussion wouldn't affect his driving. Monica suddenly panicked and bolted from the car.

Key points:

- The person must repeatedly experience intrusive imagery, such as memories, dreams, and flashbacks.

- Anniversary and/or parallel situations can trigger similar reactions.

- There must be some sort of cognitive, emotional, or physical reliving of the event.

- The person may reenact the event inappropriately.

The reexperiencing of the event must cause symptoms of withdrawal or avoidance.

"Stay with your feelings!" the therapist urged her. But every time LaTonya attempted to recall the scene, she iced over. Two years earlier, LaTonya Howard was a student at the Art Center in Des Moines. Art moved her like nothing else. Her finest moment was being chosen for a summer internship at the Museum of Modern Art in New York City. She remembered spending hours during her time off sitting in front of huge paintings by Monet and Pollock, lost in her feelings of wonder. It was after such a visit, on her way back to her apartment from MOMA, that she and her friend were jumped. When the addict found they had no money, he knifed her friend out of frustration. LaTonya held a handkerchief to stem the bleeding while her friend died on the street near the museum. For months, LaTonya was haunted by nightmares of the incident and developed an aversion to going out. Back in Des Moines she felt somewhat

safer and could attend classes and studio sessions. Something was missing, however. Several other students had asked her out since she returned, but she turned them down. Even art seemed less interesting to her. When she looked at paintings now, or tried to paint, she felt nothing.

Key points:

- Withdrawal is caused by reminders of the incident.

- Reminders can include thoughts, intrusive images, or situations.

- Reactions must present difficulties for normal living.

- The symptoms must have developed after the incident.

- Diagnosis requires at least three different kinds of withdrawal reactions (see Chapters 2 and 10 for descriptions of the types of withdrawal reactions).

Reexperience must also cause overarousal symptoms.

While visiting his friend Leon in Oregon, Andre was puzzled by the way Leon kept his yard. There were no bushes or shrubs set around the property, despite the favorable climate. The grass was kept very closely cropped, and only small flowers and ground cover stood taller than a few inches. At night Andre awoke on the couch to discover Leon sitting in the darkened living room watching quietly out the window. Bright outside lights on each corner of the house lit the entire yard. Andre got up and asked what was wrong. "Nothin', man. Go back to sleep." Andre pressed the issue, and Leon revealed that it was this way every night. Dreams of combat in El Salvador would return, and he could not go back to sleep. Leon's heart would race, and his mind would fill with images of the past and fears of imminent attack. He would have to stand watch for hours until he relaxed enough to sleep.

Leon's reactions were not proportionate to the situation. Things that would not bother others bothered him. Rapid pulse and breathing, sweating, irritability, fear, inability to concentrate—all of these are signs of overreaction if there isn't a real threat at hand. These reactions are only appropriate when a person is faced with immediate danger.

Key points:

- Overarousal symptoms appear in reaction to reminders.

- Reminders can take the form of inner experience or external situation.

- Only one such overarousal pattern is necessary to meet this criterion.

- Reactions must present difficulties for normal living.

- The symptoms must have developed after the incident.

To qualify as PTSD, this combination of intrusive imagery, withdrawal, and overarousal must persist for longer than one month. The symptoms may begin immediately after the event or may be years in the making. They may last a long time or be fairly brief. The *DSM* specifies three types of PTSD:

- *Acute*—the symptoms last less than three months

- *Chronic*—the symptoms last longer than three months

- *Delayed-onset*—the symptoms take longer to develop than six months after the incident

The *DSM* also outlines various states and conditions that are part of the PTSD picture, including relationship problems and job loss. Other conditions frequently linked with PTSD include

- feelings of guilt related to survival

- inability to control feelings

- impulsive behavior

- suicidal feelings and self-destructive behavior

- feeling disconnected from events and other people

- feelings of being constantly under threat

- hostile attitude

- physical complaints

The symptoms that add up to PTSD can be confusing, frightening, and defeating to the person who experiences them. Getting a diagnosis helps, however. It provides confirmation that there is a reason why the symptoms exist. The rationale helps us see patterns, and patterns guide treatment approaches. Once we understand why the symptoms are there and how the symptoms work together, we can plan more intelligently what to do about them. We are in a better position to find peace.

The next chapter explores the ways in which trauma symptoms can lie under the surface for years—sometimes even decades—and how those symptoms can become layered and tangled.

THINGS TO THINK AND WRITE ABOUT

- Do you suffer from intrusive memories, waking images, repetitive thoughts, or nightmares related to some incident that occurred in the past?

- Do these intrusive images—or reminders of the incident—cause you to become anxious, jumpy, fearful, angry, or painfully grief-stricken?

- Alternately, do the same images or reminders sometimes cause you to become melancholy or depressed, or to "fade out"?

- Have you felt your view of the world or of yourself shift for the worse as a result of painful experiences from your past?

- Have any of the above reactions begun since 9/11/01, or since Hurricane Katrina or other recent events?

CHAPTER 6

Serious Complications: Understanding Complex Trauma

In many ways we are driven by our personal history. Our responses to the current global uncertainty, to threats to the safety of our loved ones, and to changes in our world are colored by our learned response to threat. The greater the dangers we have encountered in the past, the more intense our response tends to be right now. For instance, a combat veteran who was traumatized in the first Gulf War and who lost friends in one of the passenger jets involved in the terrorist hijackings of 9/11 would likely experience being laid off from his job very differently from a coworker who hadn't gone through anything similar.

The concept of trauma—particularly complex trauma—helps us to make sense of our reactions to current events as well as to things that happened in the past. In addition, understanding the relationship between our past experiences and current difficulties provides us with guidance for better self-care.

Layers of Trauma from Events Past and Present

The layering of traumatic events, defined earlier in the book as *complex trauma*, creates an intricate web of symptoms. Complex trauma is made even worse when the set of traumatic incidents occurred during the formative years of childhood. A child who was molested from ages nine to thirteen, for example, endured a number of separate incidents that happened at several distinct developmental levels. This means she would have experienced each incident from a different perspective.

The case of Albert Ochoa illustrates the relationship between earlier trauma and current reactions to difficult circumstances, showing how far back traumatic history can reach. Events that happened while he was growing up shaped Dr. Ochoa's response to a workplace trauma that took place many years later. Because of childhood abuse, his symptoms after the workplace event became more than just over- or underreactivity to memories and reminders. His difficulties became focused upon his very identity:

> At age thirty-five, Albert Ochoa was a successful research chemist. He held patents on several innovative formulas and was on the verge of a breakthrough that would revolutionize electronic displays for the next five years. Then his breakthrough nearly turned into a break-down. One day his lunchroom conversation with an associate was interrupted by shouts coming from down the hall. Another associate burst into the room, shouting, "There's a fire in the lab and...." Fire in a chemical lab is always a serious emergency. Unfortunately, Albert leaped into action too soon; he grabbed a fire extinguisher and raced to the lab. Others later described the lab as a war zone, with several fires blazing, burning employees screaming, and smoke obscuring vision.
>
> As Albert burst through the double swinging doors, someone shoved him hard. He remembers having trouble shifting mental gears to the dawning realization that he was being assaulted—by another scientist, Tom Kennedy! Tom had a knife and was slashing Albert wildly. Albert clearly remembers the look on Tom's face. He recalls, "Tom didn't shout or anything; he just stared into the distance, no emotion at all, just a strange, disconnected look as he set about the business of cutting me up."
>
> Another employee, who had been held hostage, with Tom's knife to her throat, and was paralyzed with fright, reported later that she watched Albert being assaulted. "He didn't fight back or anything. He just kept asking Tom over and over, 'Why are you doing this?' " Albert finally was able to break free and escape. It took over 120 stitches to close the wounds on his head and shoulder and to sew his ear back on.
>
> Later, during trauma therapy, Albert questioned himself, uncertain why he had been unable to fight back during the attack, yet was

able to run when the time came. In the course of therapy Albert came to understand the connection between his reactions during this incident and his reactions years earlier to severe child abuse at the hands of his mother. He had been severely beaten by his mother from the time he was five years old until he was eleven. His mother suffered from multiple-personality disorder. When she switched from her normal self to her darker self, she became vicious and cruel.

"She would come at me," Albert recalled. "If I fought back she would hurt me terribly. I knew that if I ran she would catch me and kill me. The only thing I could do was to stand still and take it. I would 'disappear' and go deep into myself. I'd turn off my feelings and become invisible. It was as if I were floating above it all, watching quietly from the ceiling. The only way she couldn't hurt me was if I didn't feel."

Not feeling became Albert's way of coping with the abuse. So much so, in fact, that later he couldn't control the response. Even when he wanted to feel, he wasn't able to. Before leaving him, his first wife complained that he never stayed connected with her, that he was "never home." In therapy he couldn't recall feeling any fear during the attack at the research lab. His not fighting back was a learned reaction. Worse, it was preventing him from benefiting from trauma treatment. Every time the therapist attempted to help him confront frightening memories of the assault, Albert would shut down.

Layers of trauma from his past had complicated Albert's current crisis. He did not react to the assault with fear or anger. Instead, he walled himself off from intense feelings and from life itself. He became disconnected from the strong feelings aroused by the assault. Constantly alert for further danger, and losing sleep because of his anxiety, he was still unable to recognize his deeper feelings of fear and vulnerability. Even in therapy his feelings shut down and became inaccessible.

Albert needed to know why he had reacted to the attack the way he did. Eventually his work in trauma therapy uncovered the connection between his long history of child abuse and the way his survival mechanism worked then and now. That understanding not only relieved his self-questioning but also gave him tools to deal with his distress.

Peeling the Onion: Childhood Trauma, Sexual Abuse, and Combat

Layers of trauma—such as Albert experienced throughout his childhood—add new dimensions to a confusing set of reactions. They create reverberating patterns of "normal" traumatic stress, wherein we alternate between overreaction and shutting down. Reactions from one incident attach to other events or reminders. Our view of the world and our sense of self are affected. We come to see the world as chaotic, malevolent, and meaningless. Value seems illusory and purpose pointless. Complex trauma attacks our sense of self, resulting in a negative and distorted self-image. If you have suffered repeated traumas, particularly stemming from childhood, or prolonged trauma in early adulthood, you may experience

- deep questioning about your character and your adequacy
- distrust of yourself and your intentions
- unnecessary skepticism toward the motives of others
- deep and abiding distrust of the world in which you live
- an unwillingness to invest in long-range projects, intimacy, or commitment

These reactions are complicated and can be defeating. They do make sense, however, if you can ferret out the connections. Understanding can guide healing. Effective therapeutic approaches are available, and much can be done to manage symptoms and rebuild a sense of self. It is important for you to see these patterns as symptoms, not as fixed elements of your character or the world.

Memory Revisited

Much of the phenomenon of complex trauma can be understood by looking at the interaction between memory and development. As discussed earlier, memories of overwhelming and threatening events are stored differently than normal memories. The emotions and bodily sensations of the moment are linked with the visual memory in such a way that the memory becomes too powerful for the mind to integrate. That hot memory is stored in raw, unprocessed form. Reminders can trigger it to produce intense feelings or attempts to avoid those feelings.

Reminders of traumatic events do not evoke conscious memories—just the intense emotions, body reactions, or emergency behaviors that are linked to the original event. In other words, you can have the reactions without understanding why. This is particularly the case if the original incident occurred when you were too young to understand what was going on. Your self-concept, your well-being, and your view of the world can all be affected without your knowing why. You may simply believe that the world is appalling, that much happens that doesn't make sense, and that you are to blame.

Delayed reactions vary greatly in terms of cause, onset, and range and types of symptoms. They can become layered and debilitating. This is important, because complex trauma reactions can further confuse the way you respond to global conditions as well as to personal events. One thing we haven't yet discussed is how reactions to past events can create life themes that guide our actions. This is illustrated in Alexandra's story.

I thought I had left emergency nursing forever. But on the morning of September 11, 2001, my life changed—again! I was driving south on Route 1 past the Pentagon on the way to my job as a trauma thera-pist in Washington, D.C. Suddenly the blue sky opened up with a huge orange fireball and an enormous column of black smoke. The stoplight turned green but no one moved. The man next to me yelled, "Did you see that?" Yes, I did.

Without thinking I turned toward the dense, black smoke at the Pentagon, parked, and—wearing a beige linen suit and high heels—ran toward the fire. I wasn't thinking clearly, but I knew I had to try to help. I could see people starting to emerge from the inferno. Just yards away from the billowing black smoke and flames shooting into the sky, a lone figure struggled to set up a triage area on a grassy lawn. As I approached and identified myself, he threw me a stetho-scope and said, "Start triaging!"

I helped lay out the tarps. Several persons were brought to us. Smoke inhalation, lacerations, burns, shock—little could be done except the most basic first aid. Without ice or water and with just one tub of supplies, we did what we could, assessing, treating, and reassuring. One man with first- and second-degree burns on his hands and arms related his sense of failure to reach others. "If only I had the right card for entry or a hatchet or hammer—anything to break open the door," he said. "I heard people on the other side screaming!" I comforted him and assigned him another victim who only had a mild laceration to the forehead.

"You're buddies," I told them. "Stay together here until we clear you!"

Other medical personnel began to appear. We just continued to do what we could. I was soon festooned with rolls of surgical tape; scissors protruded from my bra; grass, dirt, and bloodstains covered the front of my once-lovely summer suit.

Complications

Then a man came running across the grass yelling that another plane was approaching—just twenty minutes out! F-16s screamed across the sky. "What the hell," I remember thinking. "We are at war!"

I shouted at the man who had assumed control that he should get everyone out of the open and under a nearby overpass, and I began to move people myself. Others joined me, rushing in to help move the equipment.

The area was becoming flooded with uniformed and nonuniformed personnel, equipment, supplies, and stretchers filled with medical debris. Helicopters began arriving. For the first time I was aware of sirens wailing and police cordoning off the area. Black vans appeared that contained large water bottles that I began to offload. I noticed FBI investigators carrying clipboards.

With so many real pros present, I decided to hand over the triage role and help the people who appeared stunned. I directed them to sit down out of the hot sun and out of view of the burning building. Three bedraggled firefighters appeared who needed to talk. They had been at the heliport and barely escaped death. Then, another pair came to join us, air-traffic controllers who had also been near the heliport at the time of impact.

One said she had been fifty feet from the wing of the plane as it went by. She remembered being thrown to the ground. Now all she wanted to do was to go back, find her purse, and get her keys and identification. I knew that wasn't possible, but I walked her toward the building. It became clear to her then that no one would get near the area—it was a crime scene—and the charred remains of her vehicle were visible.

"Okay," I said, "I am going to get you two home."

Going Home

Hours later I finally made it back to my surrealistically quiet neighborhood. I went over to my neighbor's apartment and sat fixated in front of the TV, watching images from New York, Pennsylvania, and the Pentagon. Although I lost my words for a while, I tried my best to explain to my neighbor what it was like at the Pentagon. I couldn't, so I went back to my apartment. I carefully removed my smoke-filled clothing. I folded my suit and put it on my coffee table, where it stayed for three months as a reminder of that day.

Over the next few weeks things did not return to normal. Friends and colleagues called. Are you okay? Do you need to debrief? Would you take time away from the practice to serve as a debriefing clinician? I went to Bethesda the day after the attacks to do that and more. I covered a hotline. For three weeks I debriefed victim groups. My own clients were sandwiched into my available time.

Then I just couldn't do any more. I hit the wall emotionally and physically and needed to rest. That was when I realized I had no one to turn to for my own support. I felt alienated. It seemed as though no one who hadn't been there could understand about that morning. It was an old theme for me; I'd been there before. I was isolated and in pain. At the same time, I felt incredibly grateful to find myself there; everything had come full circle. It was about my missing husband.

Held Captive by History

I met my husband thirty-five years ago in medical school, just as the war in Vietnam was building. I was training to become a nurse; he was studying to become a doctor. Tom was in the Air Force ROTC program. Not long after our marriage, he got the chance to do something he'd always wanted to do: fly a fighter plane. He was sent to Vietnam. I lived in a state of fear. During his tour he was reassigned to cargo missions in and out of small airfields. On one of his landings his plane was shot from the sky by ground fire. My husband was reported missing in action.

I couldn't deal with the loss. I was convinced he was alive. I finished nursing school and joined the Air Force as a flight nurse, thinking I could find him in Vietnam, hold him, bring him peace. I served on medevac flights in and out of Vietnam. My memories of

that time consist of blood, body parts, fear, pain, and despair. Look-
ing back, I can see that no one could have saved all those men. At the
time, however, it felt like personal failure. I was haunted by feelings
of inadequacy and despair. I felt like I was in the way. I never found
Tommy, and I lost part of myself in the process.

My grieving for my lost husband was eclipsed by the trauma I had
experienced. I couldn't let go of Tommy because I was haunted by
war. The two became intertwined and intensified by my need to
redeem myself in my own eyes. I embarked upon a career as a trauma
specialist, attempting to do for others what I couldn't do for myself
—find peace.

I felt buried alive by the memories of Vietnam—guilty for being
part of a terrible killing machine, guilty for not being better at doing
what I was sent to do. Years of accumulated guilt soaked my soul
with trauma, and I developed complex PTSD. On September 11,
2001, it seemed as though redemption had been placed in my path,
and this time I could and would make a difference. I completed the
mission I'd begun thirty years before. The opportunity to help at the
Pentagon that morning erased my years of longing to find Tommy
and to hold his hand.

For over thirty years, Alexandra had been haunted by the sudden loss
of her husband in combat and her own subsequent war experience. Then,
on September 11, 2001, she found herself in the midst of battle again.
Alexandra was propelled to act by reflexes that had been conditioned
under fire. This time, however, the outcome was very different. Questions
about her adequacy and motives that had plagued her for three decades
were laid to rest.

Troubled Times and Low-Level Traumatic Stress

For many people, 9/11 and its aftermath have disrupted their lives so
much that they experience reactions that are best understood as trauma.
This phenomenon has two dimensions. For some, the terrorist attacks
served as a reminder of prior trauma—simple or complex—and triggered
a reawakening of dormant symptoms. Veterans' hospitals, for example,
reported surges in admissions and readmissions to their PTSD programs.
Private counselors and health professionals reported increases in people
seeking their services.

For others, the events of the past several years have been traumatic in and of themselves. Many have been profoundly shaken by the attacks, by the fear of further attacks, and by the sudden deterioration of the national and international scene. The world suddenly changed for them, and they've had difficulty assimilating the changes. The angst and dislocation they feel and the agitation and fading they experience, are best described as a subclinical, low-level, traumatic stress reaction.

If any of the descriptions of trauma presented in this chapter or in Chapter 5 fit you, it is important that you stabilize your reactions and consider getting professional help. Part II of this book presents many useful tools to provide help and hope. Before moving to Part II, however, we need to look further into the more subtle and pervasive effects of exposure to uncertainty, fear, and trauma. Dealing with the constant stress of rapid change and the reactions that follow can produce a second-level set of effects. Over time we can become exhausted; we run out of gas. This second-level reaction is more spiritual in nature. It is reflected in our spirit and attitudes toward living. At this level we can become wounded just as surely as we can at the levels of emotions and body. I invite you to explore and assess this other facet in the next chapter.

THINGS TO THINK AND WRITE ABOUT

- Have you recently found yourself harboring deep questions about your character and your adequacy?

- Are you experiencing a newfound distrust of yourself and your intentions?

- Are you becoming unnecessarily skeptical about the motives of other people?

- Are you developing a deep and abiding distrust of the world in which you live?

- Do you find yourself struggling with a growing unwillingness to invest in long-range projects, intimacy, or commitment?

CHAPTER 7

Running Scared in the Brave New World: The Wounding of Spirit and Attitude

Byron Phillips stood next to me outside the high school theater during intermission. He was a lawyer in town, and his son and my daughter were in the school play being staged inside. Byron spoke quietly, with a sense of urgency and despair. "Look at these people," he said, indicating the group of other parents. "If you were up against it and your family needed a place to live for a week or two, how many of these people would take you in?"

"What do you mean," I asked, looking around.

"I mean here we are, going through the motions of being normal, but things are different. Disconnected. Where's the community? I hardly feel like I live here anymore."

Something does seem to be very wrong. The changes in our lives over the past several years have been profound. Some of our assumptions of invulnerability and unlimited capability have been seriously challenged. Even our view of ourselves as wise and morally elevated people seems questionable to many and comical to some. In many ways we have been confronted with a blow to our sense of who we are as an extended community and what we are about. On the national and global stage, this plays out in the form of political drama. In our individual lives it manifests in more personal terms: as a wounding of spirit and attitude.

Chronic Trauma, Collective Angst

Years ago sociologists coined the term *angst* to refer to a sense of dread and dislocation during the age of industrialization. As factories were built, people became less connected to their roles as members of the village. They became identified only with their particular niche in the factory and they frequently moved out of their home communities to follow their jobs. The effect on individuals and on village life was profound. People lost their grounding and sense of place; they shifted from being an integral part of an extended community to feeling like an isolated and replaceable cog in an impersonal machine.

The recent increase in terrorist acts has had a similar effect, leaving us, too, with a feeling of dread and dislocation. In the 1982 film *The Year of Living Dangerously*, director Peter Weir beautifully captures this sense of angst. Djakarta is about to explode in violence. The camera follows British attaché Jill Bryant on a bittersweet shopping trip through the local marketplace. Jill, an intelligence agent, has intercepted a message warning of an inbound arms shipment that will spark an insurgent attack. As she looks around the market at the people going about their daily shopping— a culture she loves—she alone carries the knowledge that all of it is about to change drastically and tragically.

Day after day, many of us—like Jill Bryant—look around wondering if our lives are going to remain the way they are or be swept away in a moment of chaos. We suffer from more than a set of unfortunate feelings or a collective bad mood. We are caught in a shift in attitude. Whereas moods are feelings, attitudes are opinions and are based on beliefs. A negative attitude reflects an evaluation that something is unlikely to turn out well. Unfortunately, negative beliefs and attitudes infect our actions and reactions. This can become a vicious circle, continually making things worse. Our attitudes shape our expectations, and our expectations drive our behavior. It works like this:

- Attitudes reflect our experiences and our thoughts about the future.

- Experiences shape our beliefs.

- Beliefs shape our attitudes.

- Attitudes also determine our reactions to situations and our actions in the world.

- If difficult experiences form toxic beliefs and attitudes, the result will be a perpetuation of difficult experiences.

Toxic Conditions, Toxic Beliefs

Fear and trauma can break your heart. Watching the future dim and the world deteriorate is to bear witness to a tragedy. Perhaps it would be easier if we did not have to witness the effect on our children and others we love. When we live and work under increasing threat and despair, we are subject to feelings of fear and hopelessness.

Fear is contagious. When we are afraid, others can tell. Even when we try to hide it—even when we aren't aware of it—we communicate our fear through our choices and decisions, our consumer patterns, our voting, and particularly our parenting. Because our beliefs and attitudes determine our reactions, and our reactions in turn help determine the outcome, we can poison our future with "leftovers" from the past. What we expect creates what we get.

Over time our optimism, openness, and enthusiasm can change to pessimism, cynicism, and despair. Psychologists talk about basic needs (safety, trust, self-esteem, and control) and higher-order needs (purpose, effectiveness, connection, and integrity). We can develop toxic beliefs and attitudes on both of these levels as a result of our chronic exposure to toxic conditions in our world.

Running Scared

Our attitudes determine the way we face each new day, each new experience, and each new person. They determine whether we are open to possibilities and opportunities. They make it possible for us to move into richer, more meaningful interactions and intimacy. Attitudes create the basis of our ability to be present with others and open to new life, or to shut our future down. They shape our lives.

For instance, if we believe a situation is dangerous, we typically avoid it, choke up, or become aggressive. This works so long as there is, in fact, a danger at hand. But if there is no danger, or if the danger is less than we think, things end up worse than they otherwise would have. Unless the danger is in proportion to our fear, our feelings, attitudes, and beliefs work against us. We may avoid situations that hold promise, or we may handle them poorly.

Our belief that many of our basic needs will be met has been shaken by political events over the past several years. If our sense of safety has been eroded, if we have found others or ourselves untrustworthy, or if we have found ourselves repeatedly shaken by surprising and unfortunate turns of events, we may have formed corresponding belief and attitude patterns that now work against us.

FEAR-BASED RESPONSES WHEN OUR BASIC NEEDS ARE THREATENED

Basic Needs	Fear-Based Responses
Safety: Am I safe?	I am in great danger, and so are those I love.
Trust: Whom can I trust?	I cannot trust other people.
Self-esteem: Can I believe in myself?	I am incompetent and without great value.
Connection: Can I risk intimacy with others?	Risking sharing myself with others is too dangerous.
Control: Can I relax and let things work out?	I must control whatever I can.

However well justified, these experience-driven beliefs and attitudes rob us of peace of mind and the rewards of living. They keep us from living the rich and productive lives we long for. If we remain driven by these toxic beliefs and attitudes, we will avoid or mishandle the very situations that can bring us what we want most in life: love, acceptance, happiness, and joy.

Joys of the Heart and Spirit

Sigmund Freud once said that love and work are the two most important sources of our joy and happiness. While a bit simplistic, it is an important concept. If we expand the notions of love and work beyond their normal, narrow definitions, Freud has revealed great truth. Love can be taken to include all of our relationships, including the relationship we have with our deeper self, the world, and whatever spiritual realities we perceive. Work can be seen as more than just our jobs; it includes our most meaningful activities, our purpose and mission in life. If we approach our love and work with passion, our lives will indeed bring great satisfaction.

Many of us get great satisfaction and joy out of our work. In my work supporting counselors and teachers in Lower Manhattan following the terrorist strikes on the World Trade Center, I discovered that school staff scored highly on measures of both extreme stress *and* satisfaction. While they suffered adverse conditions and personal fears—in fact, many were traumatized—they nevertheless derived personal fulfillment and contentment from meeting the needs of their students during those difficult times.

We each have higher-order needs that we seek to satisfy. These include a sense of purpose, effectiveness or personal power, connection, and integrity. Our chosen career, profession, or avocation is one way we seek to satisfy those needs. So are our various relationships.

Let's take a look at each of the higher-order needs.

Purpose

As human beings, we need to have a sense of purpose. Our relationships and our work feel pointless if there is no guiding reason behind them. Human beings are mission-driven and function best when involved in some sort of undertaking. This pursuit may involve our work, our family, or an avocation. Through a sense of purpose, our life is infused with meaning. If we lose that sense of purpose, we feel our efforts and our suffering are absurd. In taking inventory of the extent to which your higher-order need for a sense of purpose is fulfilled, you might ask yourself: Do I derive a sense of meaning and purpose in my work and my life?

Think about any beliefs and attitudes that may reflect a wounded sense of purpose. These attitudes may be carryovers from your early family experience, or they may be more recent in origin. Whatever their source, they can poison your future. Look especially for thoughts along the following lines:

- The world is random and chaotic.
- People act only in short-sighted self-interest.
- I no longer have a sense of purpose.
- It doesn't matter what I do.
- Ideals are just an illusion.

Power: The Ability to Act Effectively

While our sense of purpose guides our actions, we need to know that our efforts have some effect. Effectiveness means we have the power to act effectively in the world and to carry out our intentions. If we feel powerless to act, or if we sense that our actions will have no effect, we suffer a pervasive sense of futility and absurdity. When this happens, the balance of costs versus benefits is weighted against our motivation to persevere during hardships. We need to feel that what we do matters. Our sense of personal power—the belief that we are able to pursue our values and carry out our purpose—sustains us.

Ask yourself: In my work and relationships, am I actually carrying out the purpose I feel in my life? The following toxic beliefs and attitudes can prevent you from feeling a sense of effectiveness:

- I cannot carry out my purpose.
- My actions have no impact in the world.
- I am powerless.
- It doesn't matter what I think.
- It's foolish to dream.

Connection

We need to feel connection with others. Humans are inherently social; we are raised in families or groups, we live in the world, we join in community efforts, and we realize our highest aspirations through the support of others. Even the tallest among us stand upon the shoulders of others. Although we all need time for ourselves and we each need some degree of autonomy, nevertheless isolation leaves us incomplete. As human beings, we stand in relation to friends and family, our community and culture, our world, and our higher power. Through all of these connections, we become whole.

Toxic outlooks can reflect a breach in these connections. Ask yourself: Do I feel a strong sense of connection to others, to the world, to my deeper self, and to my higher power? Be sensitive to the following toxic attitudes and beliefs that indicate a loss of connection:

- I am isolated and alone.

- I bear no allegiance to any social group.
- I have no connection with my God or higher power.
- I have no sense of having a deeper self.
- No one really cares for me.

Integrity

Finally, our purpose, effectiveness, and relationships must be consistent with what is unique and distinctive about us as individuals. When we live with integrity we are whole and our life stands for something. Without integrity we experience our lives as disjointed and fragmented. We need to know that what we do is compatible with who we are and what we hold to be of value.

Think about this question: Is the way I am living my life—my work, my interests, my activities—consistent with who I am and what I am about? Attitudes and beliefs that indicate a collapse of personal integrity include the following:

- What I do has nothing to do with who I am.
- What I *have* defines who I am.
- It doesn't matter *how* I do what I do because the ends justify the means.
- My primary objective is to get what I want or what others have.
- Might makes right.

Assessing Spiritual Balance

If you recognize that some of these toxic beliefs and attitudes express how you feel right now, you may be struggling with a loss of spirit and joy. Each of the four areas of spiritual strength—purpose, effectiveness, connection, and integrity—can provide a sense of fulfillment and joy, or a sense of depletion and loss. Further, you can experience deep fulfillment in one area and depletion in another. Part of understanding your spiritual needs involves assessing each of the four areas of fulfillment in your life and the balance among them. The following chart will help you make that assessment and determine the areas of particular need.

Filling out this chart is simple. Each of the four areas is shaped like a wedge of pie. Use a pencil to color in each area from the center outward. If you feel that your sense of purpose, for example, is well defined and you gain satisfaction from knowing what you are about, then shade in that section from the center (0 percent fulfilled) outward to 90 percent or so. Your section would be colored in nearly to the outer edge. If you feel like you have little sense of purpose, just shade the wedge from the center outward a little way. You decide how much or how little is right for you.

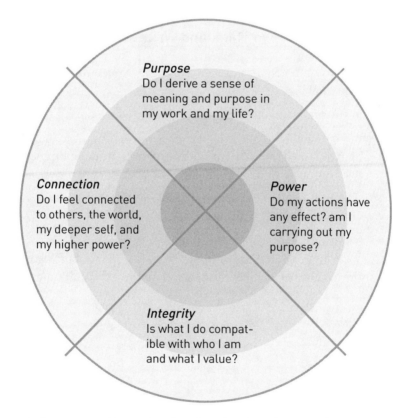

When you are finished, sit back and look at the overall picture. Is the chart mostly filled in? Are some areas fuller or emptier than others? Think about the implications of this chart while we get a little more specific about attitudes and beliefs.

As humans, we seek meaning. Our spiritual needs figure into the overall pattern of our reaction to trying times and personal crisis. Events in the world can interact with our past hurts to wound our attitudes and constrict our lives. Our sense of purpose, connection, effectiveness, and integrity are the functional building stones of spiritual health and well-being. Without them, we experience our lives as pointless, isolated, absurd, and fragmented, whatever our belief system. When fearful experiences conspire to deplete us on these levels, we must take positive and direct action to rekindle our spirit and restore our lives.

Things to Think and Write About

- Have you recently found yourself engaging in a lot of fear-based thinking?

- Do you feel that your views of the world and of yourself have changed for the worse?

- What did you discover when you assessed the areas of purpose, effectiveness, connection, and integrity?

- When you filled out your spiritual balance chart, did you notice areas that needed attention?

- Have you thought about consulting a trusted spiritual advisor regarding these matters or about beginning or revitalizing a spiritual practice to meet the demands of these difficult times?

Tools for Hope
and Healing

CHAPTER 8

Keeping It Together
when You're
Falling Apart

Part I of this book presented a foundation for understanding how overwhelming events can create lasting distress, and how recent events have created a backdrop that exacerbates the normal crises of living. In Part II we put these concepts to work. You will find that the insight you've gained about how your reactions were formed and how they have developed into life difficulties will give you the key to breaking their hold on you. Chapters 8, 9, and 10 form an "iron triangle" of practical approaches useful in dealing with

1. the alternating intense feelings and shutdown generated by our rapidly changing world

2. reactions to prior traumas and emotional states triggered by recent changes

3. specific traumas or sudden losses that are happening right now

This chapter provides you with the basics of psychological first aid. We will review the fundamentals of acute stress response and the principles used in managing extreme reactions. This information can be very helpful to you in many circumstances: during emergencies, in the midst of delayed stress reactions triggered by present situations, or whenever you find yourself reacting in ways that are counterproductive. These techniques were developed for use—and are currently being used—following terror attacks, emergencies, disasters, war, and difficult field assignments abroad. Even though they're quite simple, they have proven themselves helpful in extreme situations. They will provide you with a valuable edge during your own times of trouble. As you will see, the tools presented here are elaborated on in later chapters so they can help you deal with a wide range of situations.

The story below of J.T., a former antiwar activist, could be the story of any of a thousand returning vets who find themselves in an environment where they react to situations based on survival instincts. Her story is special, though, because later—much later—she was able to see how the skills she used helped others and how she herself was helped by the actions and concern of a stranger.

> *It was 1973 and I was like one of those returning Vietnam vets who can't take off their jungle fatigues. The fight against the war had consumed my life for years. It had provided me with purpose, meaning, a reason to get up every morning. I had been on military footing, putting personal needs aside, often working through the night, churning out leaflets, speaking at demonstrations, giving media interviews, and having sex on the run with a convenient partner the way one would wolf down a sandwich while running for the train.*
>
> *Now the war was ending; everything I had worked for was coming to pass. Even so, I felt lost and disoriented. I rattled around New York like a lone die in a felt-lined cup, looking for the game. But the game was over. I became a taxi driver, one of New York's first women cabbies. I'd get up at five every morning and walk to the cab company. If I was lucky, I'd get a cab with working brakes and windshield wipers. Most days, at least one vital function was missing. There was no radio. I chain-smoked to pass the time. Taxi drivers were easy marks for rip-off artists. I got pretty used to the shakedowns, and even became nonchalant about them. Guns, knives, one time a screwdriver. "Yeah, yeah," I'd say, rolling my cigarette between my fingers. "Take the money; get outta my cab." Well, one night I was minding my own business in a second-story, mom-and-pop bookstore in downtown Brooklyn. It was one of those leftist places where they'd have forums, talks, things like that. A meeting was going on that night. I was in the room that held the books, a semienclosed space that was separate from the meeting hall.*
>
> *A guy came in to rip off the store. I was near the cash register, and I could see that he was a junkie and was sick. He acted like he was going to buy a pamphlet. He put fifty cents on the counter. But then he took out a pistol and aimed it at my chest. "Open the cash*

register and give me the money," he said. I looked around. There was nobody who could see us, no one who could help me. I looked at the register. It was one of those big old cash registers with round keys on long, curved metal supporters. I had to push them hard to open the drawer. It opened with a "ping," and we both looked at the few dollars lying there. I could see he was becoming more desperate, shaking, drooling, in need of his next fix.

"We're gonna go inta that room, there, and you're gonna tell those people to give me their money." He waved his gun crazily, up at the ceiling, at the wall, back at me. I could see his finger tremble on the trigger.

I became super calm on the outside, evoking every maternal, soothing instinct I had in me. "Listen," I told him, "those people in there are just working stiffs. They don't have much money...."

"We're goin' in there," he insisted.

"...in fact, they're revolutionaries. Nobody's gonna call the cops, nobody has a gun; they're just gonna wanna give you the money so you can get what you need. So...how about taking the bullets out of the gun?"

He seemed suddenly docile, took out five, asked me if I wanted to hold them. "No," I answered. I didn't want to touch them, and neither did I want him to fight me for them if he decided he wanted them back. "You keep them," I said. There was still that one bullet left in the gun. "How about taking that last one out?"

Something in him snapped back at my insistence. He screamed, "No!" and grabbed my shirt at the chest, picked me up, and flung me against the wall. As I hit, a small, tearful "please" squeaked out with my breath.

We walked across the hall to the meeting room. He stood to the left side of the doorjamb, unseen by the others, keeping the gun positioned firmly under my chin. The lights seemed unnaturally bright. I felt like I was onstage in a school play, saying lines, going through motions, and not knowing how or why—completely on automatic pilot.

"Friends," I said, making sure my voice projected to the far reaches of the room, "there's a man here who wants you to give him money." Two burly guys jumped up and started making their way toward me. I thought, I'm going to die here. "No!" I said it firmly,

but not too loudly. I stretched my hands and arms out, urging them back. "He has a gun on me. Please sit down." I was in charge.

From my left, the guy peeked into the hall. He pointed out a black woman with a hat on. "Tell the sister to pass around her hat."

I pointed at her. "She will pass around her hat. Please put a dollar or two into it."

"No, all of their money!"

"I mean, all of your money."

He took the hat filled with their bills. Then he took the gun off my throat.

"Good-bye," I said.

"No, you're going downstairs with me."

I'm going to die here, I thought.

We walked down the dark stairway. At the bottom, he said, "You know, y'all are all right. Maybe when I clean myself up, I'll come back here and help out."

"No, don't ever come back," I told him. "Take the money and go. Take care of yourself." He went out. I turned the dead bolt. He was gone. I was alive.

I walked back up the stairs. There was a beat or two of silence, and then the meeting resumed. I sat in the back of the room for a few minutes before what had just happened began to sink in. I stood up and walked alone to another room. I sat down at a small desk, and started to cry.

I heard a low shuffle at the door. I looked up and saw there was a young woman approaching me. She put a hand on my forearm. "That must have been awful," she said. "Are you all right?" I nodded and tried to smile. For many years I dismissed the incident, just as most of the others in that room did. To a couple of folks, I became legendary. "J.T.'s hard," they'd say, laughing. Looking back, I recognized that I did what I did out of good instincts—to preserve my life. At least there was only one bullet in the gun. That the one bullet would have been for me is something I couldn't fully accept for maybe twenty years afterward. I also came to understand that at that time of my life, my own survival did not seem very important. Maybe that's why I brushed off the significance of the event for so long.

I remembered and started to tell this story as an example of how we make meaning of traumatic events. I was training people in how

*to help others after a critical incident, and all of a sudden it made
sense to tell it.*

*What I say about it is this: I will always remember the day a guy
held a gun to me, the day I almost lost my life. I will remember how a
crowd of people then acted as if nothing had happened. But I will
also always remember that someone—one person—made a kind,
human gesture and touched me, asked me if I was okay. And that has
also become part of this memory.*

*This story has stopped being something that belongs just to me. It
has transformed into a tool I use to help others understand what
happens to us in life-threatening situations, and how they can help
others to withstand and recover from them. I can think of no better
use for it.*

Losing It

When bad things happen, it is normal for people to feel fear, anger, and
sadness. Who hasn't experienced events that left them with difficulty
focusing and thinking or feeling overwhelmed and defeated? Most of the
time we struggle through these unfortunate moments in spite of our reactions. We emerge with our sense of our strengths and abilities reasonably
intact. I hope this has been your experience.

It isn't always that way, unfortunately. Sometimes we don't do so
well—or at least not as well as we would like to. Circumstances are too big,
too frightening, too threatening for us to handle. In these situations we
cannot cope. Our reactions morph into the following extreme versions of
themselves:

- Fear turns into panic.
- Anger turns into rage.
- Crying turns into hysteria.
- Difficulty focusing and thinking turns into "fading."
- Being overwhelmed turns into an inability to respond.
- Trouble knowing what to do turns into paralysis.

Meltdown is never pretty. When we fall apart, we lose control of ourselves and of the situation. Worse than that, we may lose respect for our-

selves. We may be ashamed of how we acted, and we may begin to fear the world.

> *Walter Clark failed to see the other car until it was too late. Coming from nowhere, it suddenly was upon him. Walter remembers that it seemed to slow down before it hit the side of his car, yet he was unable to make his body move fast enough to avoid the collision. After the impact, events seemed to race ahead. Onlookers suddenly appeared, then police, then medical people. Walter found himself standing there listening to these people talk, though what they said didn't make much sense. Finally someone suggested that he lie down on the gurney. Later he learned he'd been there for over an hour. It had seemed like only a few minutes. It was hours before the hospital would release him, and then only after his daughter was notified and picked him up. They kept saying that he was experiencing something like "psychological shock."*

Recall the discussion of the two types of acute stress response: agitated ASR and faded or shutdown ASR. Walter experienced the shutdown type of acute stress response. Whether it is the shutdown or the agitated variety, acute stress response can occur in crisis situations that present threat. It also can occur as a part of a delayed reaction to a trauma that occurred in the past. Reminders of threatening situations can create the same reactions that the person experienced at the time of the crisis. *External* events, such as similar places, people, or situations, can trigger an acute stress response. *Internal* events, such as memories, flashbacks, or nightmares, can do the same. Sometimes we are not even aware of the specific cue that triggers an acute stress reaction, but it is there anyway!

> *For months after the accident, Walter was fearful when driving. The worst times were when cars approached from cross streets as he was driving through intersections. He would notice them slowing to stop, but it seemed like they would be unable to stop in time to avoid hitting him. Sometimes they appeared to lurch ahead and be about to hit him. They never did, but each time it happened Walter panicked and hit his brake, then for the next several blocks he was in a daze. Sometimes he couldn't recall what had transpired from the time he was scared until the time he got home. Not only had he experienced an acute stress response when he was hit, now he was*

*suffering from delayed stress reactions identical to those he'd
endured at the time of his accident.*

Both forms of acute stress response pull us away from the present
moment. If we have an *overreaction* to crisis or to trauma reminders, we
lose ourselves to the world of external threat. We become ineffective
because of our wild panic, seething rage, or unbearable grief or horror. If
we have an *underreaction* to the crisis or reminder, we become lost in
retreat. We go too deeply into ourselves, focusing mostly on our personal
reactions—our confusion and helplessness. Our ability to take action is
compromised. This is what happened to Walter in the days and weeks following his auto wreck: The presence of other cars on the road seemed such
a great threat that he panicked and then "spaced out" when he encountered one. Under such circumstances, pulling ourselves back into balance
is critical. The purpose of staying psychologically present in a hostile environment is to allow us to cope with the situation.

We need to learn ways of coping with acute stress reactions when they
occur. If we can develop the skills to remain psychologically present, we
can use them in the following two ways:

1. In dealing with reactions to emergencies

2. In dealing with delayed stress reactions of an acute nature

The Range of Our Response to Crisis

Acute stress responses represent the two extremes of a wide range of reactions to crisis situations. This range extends from no reaction on one end
of the continuum to maximum reaction on the other. It is useful to divide
the range into the following seven degrees:

1. Acute stress shutdown

2. Faded

3. Objective

4. Fully present

5. Involved

6. Overreactive

7. Acute stress agitation

RESPONSE CONTINUUM

Each response level shapes how we experience the world and ourselves in the world. We see things through the filter of our thoughts and feelings. When these change, so does the world we see. Each position on the response range colors how the world looks to us.

Position	What it feels like	How the world looks
1. Shut down	No feeling	Disconnected, surreal
2. Faded	Things don't seem important	Out of control
3. Objective	Calm	Serious but understandable
4. Fully present	Wide range, moderate feeling	Not good but understandable
5. Involved	Anger, fear, sadness	Dangerous
6. Overreactive	Overwhelming feeling	Out of control
7. Agitated	Unbearable feeling	Unendurable

Comfort-Zone Positions: Objective, Fully Present, and Involved

Position number 4, "fully present," is midway between the two extremes. Like a martial arts expert in a state of readiness, sizing up a situation before stepping either back or forward, this middle position represents a waiting stance. Being fully present means being aware of what is going on and reacting in a way that is neutral, emotionally available, controlled, and ready to act. It is a position of great emotional resilience and affords the most flexibility of options.

Positions number 3 and 5 are each one step away from neutral. Being "involved" is a move toward personal engagement with the situation. This can mean feeling emotionally connected and invested. It involves emotions such as anger, fear, sadness, excitement, or joy. Involvement also allows flexibility of action; one can take any number of direct actions or none at all. Being "objective" is a move back from being fully present. It is an attempt to keep perspective and control. Emotions are kept in check. Actions may be taken, but tend to be minimal. Objective observers try to see things from other perspectives and refrain from "siding" with any one person's point of view.

Which is the preferred position? It depends. Sometimes it is best to remain in an objective state of mind, one step removed. Sometimes personal involvement is called for by the circumstances or one's values and beliefs. All three positions are flexible and adaptive, and all three use emotions to help the individual appreciate the situation and to inform judgment.

The Danger Zones: Fading and Overreaction

Both faded and overreactive (positions 2 and 6, respectively) are more extreme. When objectivity turns to fading, flexibility and the ability to act effectively are greatly reduced. Fading represents a dulling of the senses and a shift of focus away from the situation. The world looks out of control. In response, the mind begins to give up attempts to monitor and change the situation. Attention turns inward and emotional response grows numb. This is an internal "circling of the wagons."

> *Tom and Suzie weren't good at handling conflict together. Tom's family had rarely raised their voices to one another; his parents had actually separated for several months following their only loud fight. This had unsettled Tom greatly at the time and he no longer trusted confrontation. Whenever Suzie confronted him, he backed off. Sometimes she responded by becoming even more aggressive. Tom found this overwhelming and would lose his ability to respond. His feelings became numb and he grew unable to talk or even think clearly. He would finally have to leave. Tom faded in the face of difficult experience, and it was costing him his relationship.*

The opposite danger is when personal involvement becomes overreaction. When a situation appears out of control, emotions take over. The attempt to monitor and change things becomes frantic. Fear, anger, or sadness predominate and drive actions. Judgment is compromised, as is the ability to direct action effectively. The overreactive person becomes preoccupied with emotion, unaware of the extent to which feelings color his or her perception of the incident.

> *Tom's fading made Suzie crazy. What began as a simple disagreement or perceived slight would set her off and end up creating a catastrophe. Suzie's family had been highly verbal, highly involved. If a problem arose, they stuck to it until it was resolved. To Suzie, that's what love meant. She interpreted Tom's silence and retreat as a sign of his rejecting her and would become anxious. Her response—"because she loved him"—was to confront him and push even more for the connection she sought. She brought up old issues and questioned his love. She pulled the children into the dispute. When he fled, it only made things worse. Sometimes she pursued him in the car or followed him to his workplace to try to straighten things out.*

Fading and overreaction pull us away from the balanced, adaptable position of being fully present. Neither is comfortable; neither is helpful in terms of being effective in changing the situation. Yet, neither should be considered a sign of psychological damage.

That is not the case with the two extreme reactions, shut down and agitated (positions 1 and 7 on the continuum, respectively). They are counterproductive and pathological.

Acute Stress Shutdown: How It Looks and Feels

The extreme form of disengagement is acute stress shutdown. It represents a psychological disconnection from the situation in response to an immediate crisis or to delayed reactions to a crisis. Another way to describe this form of ASR is *psychological shock*. You become so overwhelmed by the situation that you can no longer respond, no longer think constructively, and no longer act. One state it produces is called *dissociation*, a condition in which you do not identify with either being there or even with being yourself. This loss of a sense of self is accompanied by an experience of the world as surreal or strange.

The world loses its sense of reality and its sense of order. Events appear to be disconnected; things look unreal. Because thought processes have slowed, external events appear to speed up. Similarly, the sense of self is impaired. Memory and anticipation blur.

Given this impairment, it is hard to stay aware when you are shutting down. Some clues that you have entered a state of shutdown include the following:

- Others say things to you that imply underreaction on your part, such as "Hey! Pay attention!" "Stay focused!" "Are you all right?"

- Others suddenly appear before you and speak loudly to you.

- Things seem surreal or disconnected, or they don't seem to make sense.

- Others seem to be overreacting, given your perception of the seriousness of the situation.

- Others seem to be agitated or responding too quickly.

- Time seems to be going too quickly.

Acute Stress Agitation: How It Looks and Feels

The extreme form of engagement is acute stress agitation. The world seems all too real when you are experiencing an agitated response to a crisis. With your thinking and feeling accelerated, you become lost in the flow of events. Adaptive and creative action is impossible. Overcompensation and undirected activity compromise safety and the ability to act effectively. Feelings are intense, resulting in hysteria, panic, or rage.

This set of reactions obviously presents problems. In emergency situations, if you are extremely agitated you cannot direct your action effectively to protect your life and property. In situations where the agitation is in response to delayed stress reminders, you are unable to carry out normal functions appropriately.

Given how overwhelming events seem, it is hard to be aware when you have gone into a state of agitation. Your emotional reactions and behavior seem warranted by the extreme situation. Some clues that you are impaired include the following:

- You experience feelings of panic, rage, or overwhelming emotion.

- Your perception of the situation becomes overwhelming.

- Others make statements or ask questions that imply an overreaction on your part, such as "Hey, slow down!" "Get a grip!" "What's the matter?"

- Others fail to act in a manner that fits your perception of the seriousness of the situation.

- Others seem to be acting in slow motion, or not responding quickly enough.

- Time seems to be going too slowly.

What to Do: Tools for Managing ASR

Whether they are caused by an emergency or by delayed stress reactions, acute stress responses can be frightening and defeating. Fortunately, in such cases you can take positive action to intervene for yourself and for others. The overall approach—depending upon the type of reaction—involves the following two basic strategies:

1. If you are overreacting or agitated, you must move toward *less* engagement with the situation.

2. If you are fading or shutting down, you must move toward *more* engagement with the situation.

If you find yourself reacting from either extreme position, there are a number of things you can do. Rather than trying them willy-nilly, though, it is helpful to organize them according to steps. Acute stress response involves loss of attention, emotional extremes, physical disruption, and behavioral instability. Recovery from ASR requires refocusing your response away from these extremes onto a middle ground. Your attention and thoughts—that is, your cognitive response, as opposed to your emotional, physical, and behavioral responses—are the most responsive and adaptive, so that is the best place to begin. Once you can refocus your attention onto the present, you are in a position to restabilize your feelings and adjust your physical response. Only then can you redirect your actions more appropriately to the situation.

To intervene in ASR, then, your approach should follow this progression: First address thoughts, then feelings, then physical reactions, and finally behavior.

STEPS FOR INTERVENING IN ASR	
Level	*Goal*
1. Thoughts	Focus attention
2. Feelings	Stabilize feelings
3. Body	Adjust pacing
4. Behavior	Direct action

Note that this same general progression should be followed whether you're dealing with fading/shutdown or overreaction/agitation. *How* you apply the steps will depend upon which end of the spectrum you're dealing with.

Some suggestions for following the progression appear below. The specific strategies you use will depend upon the specific situation, but they fall into a number of general areas. They are organized following the progression from thoughts to feelings to body to behavior. Sometimes the approaches suggested address more than one domain, and sometimes several approaches can be used simultaneously. The progression outlined here is simply a general rule.

Focus

During a crisis, attention and concentration can become lost. They may be absorbed in the external event or in the reminder of a previous event. Or, they can be focused exclusively upon inner realities. Regaining control requires shifting your focus back to a balance.

What to do: Work at ignoring memories and anticipation; stay in the present moment. Question your own interpretation of the events you see. Ask yourself, "Might I be mistaken in what I see?" Understand that feelings color how you see events. Clear your head and look again.

Self/other talk

We talk to ourselves constantly, creating a running narrative of events. The words we choose to describe things change how we see them. Stated another way, our language shapes our expectations, and our expectations in turn guide our reactions.

What to do: Use clear language. When you describe things, avoid "catastrophizing." Don't use extreme words when normal words will do. Talk to yourself in calming ways. Use reminders like "Remember to think"; "Things will work out"; "Stay focused and stay strong." Talk to others if possible. Ask how they see things. Notice whether their actions show distress. If not, ask yourself what they know that you don't.

Imagery

Mental pictures guide our actions and our responses. Professional athletes include mental rehearsal as part of their training. Images created by our memory or our imagination are prime shapers of how we see the situation. This can be reversed. You can intentionally create mental images to help you cope. You can use mental pictures to calm yourself or push yourself into action.

What to do: To *calm* your agitated response, imagine relaxing scenes, such as a safe place, walking by the ocean, or sitting in the mountains smelling pine and feeling the warm sun and gentle breeze. To *increase* your response rate, imagine yourself taking action and working effectively to correct what is going wrong. Imagine yourself standing back from the situation and seeing it from different perspectives, with different outcomes.

Feelings

Emotions, thought processes, and bodily reactions are interdependent. Besides being affected by thought processes and physical reactions, feelings also steer those processes. It is important to keep in touch with your feelings and work with them. Feelings can be shaped. They can be intensified or softened. You can work with them by changing your thoughts and by changing your body reactions.

What to do: Question your feelings. Think about other possible feelings you could have. Practice feeling those instead of the ones you are feeling. Explore making your feelings more intense, then less intense. Acknowledge the feelings that are there, and then set them aside temporarily. For example, if you're feeling on the verge of panic, talk yourself down by telling yourself, "I can choose to feel differently" or "I've been through worse than this before" or "I can rise above this." Seek out someone to talk to about what you are feeling. Often other people can give us a more balanced perspective when we're feeling hostage to strong emotions.

Breath

Breath drives physical reactions. Through changing your breathing patterns, you can change your thoughts, emotional state, and physical reactions.

What to do: To lower your level of reaction, make your breathing slower, deeper, and more deliberate. A good way to do this is to breathe in units of four. Begin by taking a breath so deeply into your abdomen that your stomach extends. It is important to push your stomach out (yes, even though your mother or drill instructor always told you not to!). Breathe in for a count of four. Then hold the breath for another four count. Next, let it out slowly for a count of four. Then hold it out for a count of four. Repeat the process four times. Each time you do this, you compress a nerve in your abdomen that sends a relaxing signal to the brain. This initiates the *relaxation response* (the opposite of the *fight-or-flight response*). We will call this technique the "four-count protocol."

Alternatively, you can change your breathing pattern in order to energize your body and mind. Simply take several quick, panting breaths ("quick breaths"). Both of these techniques alter the oxygen level in your system. They send a signal to your brain saying either that things are okay and you can relax (four-count protocol), or that you need to get moving (quick breaths).

Bodily pacing

Our bodies follow a rhythmic pace. The pace reflects heart and breathing rates, brain function, and general response time. The pace shows itself in our movements, posture, and gestures. Pacing also influences our response level. We can change our response level by altering our body's pacing.

What to do: To focus your thoughts and control feelings that threaten to spiral out of control, intentionally slow down your body movements. Make your motions more deliberate and intentional. Slow your speech patterns. Rehearse what you are going to say before saying it. Leave the situation for a few minutes, if you can, to get a change of scenery. Make yourself walk slowly, and notice how your body feels. On the other end of the spectrum, to "wake yourself up"—that is, to mobilize your thoughts and get in touch with your feelings—pick up your pace. Get up and move. Make yourself do things. When you walk, deliberately walk faster than feels appropriate. Swing your arms. Remember to breathe.

Body awareness

Our bodies drive our feelings and our minds. By becoming more aware of your body—how it is feeling and what it is doing—you can pull yourself back to the present moment. Both forms of ASR operate by linking feelings to arousal level. By changing your body awareness and taking certain bodily actions, you can affect the feeling/arousal level.

What to do: During agitation, the body is jerky and hyperactive. Redirecting your body energy to more deliberate, productive tasks allows that energy to dissipate. For instance, you might move furniture around, do yard work, or find some other heavy task to do that you have been putting off. During shutdown, on the other hand, the body is inert, awaiting direction and conserving energy. Stretching, moving around, and taking purposive action allow the energy to flow again. An example of purposive action might be finding something that needs to be done, even if it is not directly relevant to the situation. Straighten your desk or the room. Wash dishes. Ask someone if you can do something to help them. Identify areas of tension in your body and stretch those areas. Moderate exercise is helpful, if the situation allows it.

In addition, no matter at which end of the ASR spectrum you find yourself, take food and liquid according to their effects on your body rather than to satisfy cravings. This might mean avoiding caffeine if you're feeling overstimulated. It might also mean stopping to eat when you're hungry. Skipping meals can cause significant fluctuations in your blood-sugar levels, which in turn can make your mood, frame of mind, outlook, and perception present a much bleaker picture than the reality. Finally, it might mean avoiding mood-altering substances. Alcohol, to name just one example, is a strong depressant. It's also important during times of high stress to provide your body with a good balance between rest and physical activity.

Ritual

For thousands of years human beings have found power in ritual. Ritual guides awareness, balances emotions, and focuses energy. Some rituals are used to mobilize energy to face challenges. Others bring comfort and a sense of community support. Some people use prayer, meditation, exercise, dance, or music. Others visit places that are significant to them.

Some get together with other people. Others find that solitude offers the best opportunity for recentering themselves.

What to do: Develop a few brief, personal rituals for both calming and raising your response levels. Use them according to the situation, and let them work for you.

Action

The whole point of thoughts and feelings during an emergency is to guide action. Conversely, actions can guide thoughts and feelings. Whether directed by yourself or others, actions and activities can be used to manage your acute stress response.

What to do: Some actions are simple and obvious. For example, remove yourself from visual and auditory contact with the emergency situation. Tell yourself, "Take a walk," or, "Sit down and take a few deep breaths." Other actions are more complex: "Take this box to that person"; "Organize these papers"; "Pack these lunches." Because your mental faculties may be impaired and your emotional control thin, activities must be within the range of your ability at the time. The purpose of the action is twofold, however: to appropriately direct your energy and focus, and to reestablish a sense of control and self-worth.

These strategies can be shaped into a personal plan. Experiment until you find which work best for you. Keep in mind that they follow the order of thoughts, feelings, body, and behavior, and they are used differently for agitated or shutdown reactions. More information about handling acute stress response is provided in the Emergency Guide located at the front of the book.

Remember, however, that if you have acute stress reactions, whether they are the result of an emergency or chronic exposure to stressful conditions, or are a delayed response to trauma, they are a sign that you need more support. Take your reactions seriously and take care of yourself for the long run.

THINGS TO THINK AND WRITE ABOUT

- Have you experienced acute stress reactions either to current situations or as delayed reactions to previous difficult circumstances?

- Have others you know had similar reactions?

- Have you considered drawing up a personal plan—following the techniques presented in this chapter—for dealing with such reactions when they happen again?

- Can you see the connection between those reactions and distrusting yourself?

- Have you explored the Emergency Guide at the front of this book? Was it helpful?

CHAPTER 9

Letting Go of Fear, Anger, and Loss

Many people walk through life burdened with simmering anger, paralyzing fear, or feelings of insurmountable loss. These feelings seem to lie in wait just below the surface and spring forth whenever the chance arises. Sometimes a social situation can trigger the reaction; sometimes even a movie or a book can do so. When these old feelings come up—like the proverbial camel's nose under the side of the tent—they take over. We are caught up again in the reactions, feelings, and thoughts we had in response to events that took place long ago.

Overreaction creates havoc in our lives. Whether we are plagued with crushing fear, uncontrollable anger, or overwhelming sadness, our lives go on hold for the duration. Sometimes our overreaction even reaches the intensity of acute stress. We can't function normally. How can you cross the river when your emotional boat is swamped?

If you are struggling with these aftereffects of overwhelming events, you are probably fed up with your life being jerked around. Why don't these symptoms just go away? Do they serve some function? How do you let go of recurrent bouts of fear, anger, and loss so that you can go on living? These are the sorts of issues addressed in this chapter. The next chapter, "Dealing with Withdrawal, Numbing, and Depression," focuses on the symptoms that lie at the other end of the spectrum.

A Quick Review of the What and Why of Arousal

The "what" question is the easy part. Several of the things we've talked about come together here. The arousal symptoms of delayed stress reactions were discussed in earlier chapters, and overwhelming feelings of fear, anger, and loss are among them. You don't need to have a diagnosed case of PTSD to suffer from repeated and overwhelming waves of anger, fear, or sadness. The normal buffeting of life events will do.

Explaining the "why" of chronic and troubling anger, fear, or sadness takes a little longer. Remember the discussion in Chapter 4 of how the mind attempts to integrate critical experiences? This process is what instigates arousal responses. And do you remember the part in Chapter 3 about brain chemicals? The connection between emergency memory and the body's alarm system explains why the arousal responses are so intense. The mind repeatedly attempts to make sense of intense memories. This in turn triggers acute stress arousal reactions long after the event.

In 1951, the first commercial computer was produced. Compared to today's desktops, UNIVAC I was huge. Silicon technology hadn't been invented yet, so the beast worked on the same large vacuum tubes and thick wiring that were used in bulky tabletop radios at the time. And it was slow! Technicians would program in equations and then go home. UNIVAC would cook all night and spit out an answer the next morning. The human mind is like that when it tries to make sense of the unthinkable. It takes a while.

While this processing is going on, the brain's emergency response system is on full alert for further danger. At any hint of trouble—from outside or inside—it overresponds. That's why reactions of fear, anger, and loss persist and can become unmanageable.

It can take a long time for the human mind to process trauma. Feelings following a trauma can become so deeply ingrained that they seem to be a personality trait poisoning all aspects of life. Arousal reactions can become entrenched habits that must be changed if we are to rediscover peace. It helps to know that a natural process underlies these feelings and that our reactions to them are essentially emergency responses. We gain direction from that knowledge.

Going to Extremes

Being mad, sad, or glad during normal times is normal. Feeling rage, hysteria, or panic during extreme, life-threatening events is also normal. But becoming enraged, hysterical, or panicked during *normal* times is neither normal nor healthy. If this is occurring in your life, you undoubtedly feel victimized by your own feelings.

We have to be reminded that how we feel is very much up to us. It is tempting to give up this control, especially when we have learned how overwhelming life's experiences can be. Because emotions are part of the brain's survival programming, we resist overriding them. Yet extreme reactions to normal life stressors can be managed. We can use the same techniques used to manage acute stress response to calm rage, hysteria, or panic that occurs long after the incident.

The Basics of Managing ASR

In Chapter 8 we outlined an approach to managing acute stress response that included intervention at the levels of thought, emotions, body, and behavior. Recall that managing the overarousal form of ASR includes the following goals:

- Refocus your attention inward.
- Shift your thoughts.
- Attend to the present.
- Lower your oxygen levels.
- Initiate the relaxation response.
- Lower your activity levels.
- Redirect your activity toward something useful.

The goals are the same for managing debilitating bouts of delayed-stress anger, fear, and sadness that are triggered by posttrauma reminders, thoughts, and arousal responses.

What Can We Do?

Before you can plan how to intervene in these cycles of overreaction, you need to understand them. You might grab a pen and paper and write down your answers to the following questions. In the days and weeks to come, as you reflect on these questions and observe yourself with them in mind, continue writing about your insights.

First, instead of focusing on why your reactions show up or how bad they are, begin by determining *where* and *when* your reactions occur. What is the context? What are the triggering conditions? Listing the "whens and wheres" provides clues about specific moments when you can begin to take countermeasures, even before reactions start.

Next, ask yourself, "Do I typically experience signs of an impending reaction?" Do you simply find yourself suddenly in the middle of a full-blown reaction, or does the reaction build gradually and predictably? If you remain aware of your internal reactions, can you see them develop? If you do, then you can take countermeasures in the early stages of fear, anger, or sadness rather than letting them develop into panic, rage, or hysteria.

Look at the nature of your reaction. How do you interpret the triggering situation and your responses to it? How do you characterize and describe these situations and responses to yourself? In what ways do your feelings follow from your thoughts and language? Are there ways in which you could shift your thoughts in order to shift your attitude? Might this attitude readjustment shift your subsequent reactions? Could you give yourself reminders and instructions that could change your emotional and physical reactions?

Are there steps you could take to moderate your body's response to the feelings or even change the feelings themselves to a less acute level? Of course there are; they are outlined in Chapter 8. The key is to plan them in advance and practice doing them. If you tend to "go blank" during your arousal reactions, try outlining your management plan on a small card and carrying it with you.

Incorporate these considerations into a personal emergency plan. Chart your cycle of overreaction on a diagram. Fill in specific countermeasures (suggested below) that you can use to intervene at each step when you feel you are losing control. A few lines from a sample emergency action plan are provided later in this chapter.

Countermeasures for Episodes of Emotional Overreaction

Moderate circumstances require moderate countermeasures, and extreme circumstances may demand extreme countermeasures. The countermeasures you adopt must be flexible and appropriate to the stage of your reaction. In other words, it's better to take countermeasures at each step of your cycle of overreaction to redirect the reaction back toward normalcy.

Here is a range of countermeasures that track the goals listed above. They are arranged to follow the progression from thoughts to feelings to body processes to behavior, as described in Chapter 8. For more explanation of how to use these techniques, review the section in that chapter titled "What to Do: Tools for Managing ASR."

— Learn how your exposure to certain external situations triggers certain reactions. Avoid such situations if necessary and if possible; this may mean, for example, walking away from a conflict with your spouse that seems like it might spiral into a major fight. But, later, when you're calm, you need to set aside time to come back and deal with the conflict. (See Chapter 11, "Stabilizing Our Children and Families," for more about making a plan for disengaging and then reengaging.)

— Distract or redirect your thoughts when they cycle into negativity. Refocus your awareness to the positive aspects of the situation. If trying to find something positive about the situation seems artificial, at the very least you can refocus your awareness from a negative state to a more neutral one. One way to do this is to replace your spiraling thoughts with a focus on an inner quality you'd like to manifest, such as peace. Repeat over and over to yourself an affirmation like, "I now return to a peaceful, grounded state." Fully engage your mind in thinking about the words as you say them.

— Refocus your awareness away from the past or future to the present.

— Use positive and calming "self-talk" reminders and encouragement.

— Set short-term goals for getting through the immediate moment.

— Use the four-count breathing technique outlined in Chapter 8.

— Walk around, or use other movements to shift your body from "alert" to "relaxed" status.

— Examine your impulse to take action (the fight-or-flight response).

— Redirect your actions toward useful activity.

Again, each of these measures is explained more fully in Chapter 8 and in the Emergency Guide. Incorporate these into your planning, but don't expect an immediate turnaround. Learn from each episode and fine-tune your plan. Most importantly, don't give up! It takes a while— sometimes a long while—to relearn how to manage reactions that have gone out of control. Be patient and be persistent. Reclaiming your life is worth it!

People who suffer from delayed reactions to overwhelming events typically have more difficulty with one of the three: rage, panic, or hysteria. The general approach outlined above can be tweaked for each. Special considerations for adapting countermeasures for each kind of reaction are discussed in the rest of the chapter.

A few lines from your personal emergency plan might look like this:

IF I... Realize my thinking is turning negative...
I WILL... Name three positives in the situation, or replace my thought patterns with a neutral mindset.

IF I... Find myself thinking about the past or future...
I WILL... Pay attention only to what is here and now.

IF I... Start telling myself, "Here we go again..."
I WILL... Tell myself, "Stay focused," and, "This could be much worse," and, "I can do this."

IF I... Start to get agitated...
I WILL... Pay attention to my breathing.

Special Case: When Resentment Keeps Exploding into Rage

You're driving to the airport. You're catching the last flight out tonight and you are speaking at a big conference tomorrow morning. Security lines have been long lately and you must be at the check-in counter well before departure time. Because your children needed extra reassurance, it took longer than expected to drop them off. Then the line at the gas station was longer than it's ever been. You'll still probably make it on time. Then traffic starts piling up. The freeway is moving sluggishly. You're becoming seriously concerned. As you round a corner, you are confronted with a sea of brake lights. It looks like the mother of all traffic jams.

Upset? Probably. Angry? Most likely. Normal? Most assuredly. But what if you find yourself going ballistic—shaking your fist and shouting obscenities at the car ahead of you, pounding on the steering wheel and laying on the horn, or perhaps pulling over to the right and racing along the shoulder, endangering yourself and others? Anger issues? Most definitely.

Deep-seated anger can lie dormant and erupt violently into rage whenever it gets the chance. It can sabotage our best efforts and kill our most important dreams. Overtaken by underlying resentment and explosive anger, we can trash our careers, our relationships, and our peace of mind. Worse, without meaning to, we can end up badly hurting those we love the most.

Letting go of anger is critical to our well-being. To do so we have to be able to understand and deal with the underlying hurt; we also must find a way to contain our outbursts of rage. Let's look at both issues.

Looking Behind the Rage

If you are plagued with rage, you probably suffered an insult to your sense of dignity and self-esteem, either recently or at some important point earlier in your life. All the self-control in the world can't address that. It may be helpful for you to deal with the matter head-on, but do so at a time when you are calm. If you have been wounded, you need all of your energy and control to deal with the issue effectively. Here are some things to consider when doing so.

What's behind your pattern of rage today? Something about certain external situations triggers your anger. During the initial traumatic incident something may have provoked strong feelings of anger you were unable to express or act on at the time. Look for any underlying injustice you suffered. Do the situations now triggering your angry feelings in any way parallel the original incident?

Another cause may be feelings of being threatened. Anger is one primitive response to something that threatens our well-being. Do the situations that set you off now resemble or remind you of a threat in the original incident?

A third possibility is that, if your primary emotional response at the time was anger upon which you were unable to act, your body may have "memorized" that pattern of anger. This is related to the first cause but differs in that the first is about frustrated emotions, while this is about physical energy patterns, and we are often less consciously aware of the latter. Sometimes our bodies hold a physical pattern of tension—in this case the readiness to strike out at a threat—until it is released. Current stressful situations may mobilize that pattern of readiness.

If you can identify what underlies your anger, you have a better chance of coming to grips with it. Sometimes it takes a while to figure out where the anger is coming from and what to do about it. Working with a counselor or therapist may be helpful. Writing about the underlying situation may be useful. The writing exercises included in the "Things to Think and Write About" sections of this book will help you prepare to take advantage of your time with a counselor by putting your experiences into a clearer form.

Tweaking Your Anger Plan

In addition to dealing with the wound underlying the anger, you can adapt the countermeasures listed above and use them to deal with the seemingly uncontrollable rage you experience today. The first step is to identify your pattern of rage. If you have a problem with anger, you most likely have considerable experience with it. Think about five of your worst episodes. What did they have in common? Look for the times and places most likely to trigger anger. Is there a train of thought or certain memories that precede your outbursts? Are some situations more likely to get to you?

Understanding anger can help diffuse anger cycles. Whenever the cycle occurs, however, you have to take direct action. The following are some practical suggestions for dealing with episodes of anger that are escalating toward rage:

Back off when you can. If the person or situation can be avoided while you are feeling extreme anger, do so. Reapproach the person or issue later, when you have regained control. At that point, you can deal with the matter more constructively. A cooling-off period can help you mobilize your higher resources.

Recognize that some situations—traffic, for example—are unavoidable. If you can't back off, use breathing, imagery, and self-talk to bring your arousal back down to a manageable level. Understand that you are not wrong to feel the anger; it's just counterproductive. Find which of the acute stress response management strategies (from Chapter 8) work best for you.

Use your head! Practice seeing the situation from other perspectives. Refuse to allow yourself the luxury of striking out—verbally or physically. When you are in an anger episode, don't let your feelings determine what is warranted, permissible, or desirable. Have an escape strategy available so that you have an alternative to taking actions that are driven by rage.

When to Get Help

Is your plan working? If so, wonderful! It is an ongoing process, so keep at it. If it isn't working, you might benefit from assistance in the form of therapy or counseling with a qualified mental-health professional. You *definitely* should get help under any of the following circumstances:

- When you have trouble restraining yourself from acting on your anger
- When your anger is causing your relationships at home or at work to suffer
- When you are self-medicating with alcohol, drugs, food, or compulsive behavior
- When you are just plain sick of your feelings pushing you around

Take this stuff seriously. Holding on to resentment and rage keeps you focused on the past; it cuts you off from living in the present and building the future. It creates an internal chemistry that is harmful to your body over time. Dealing with injustices and blows to your dignity is important. But the past is over. Fighting old battles is important only to the extent that they still live. It is important to exercise the power to discern the living from the dead.

To refer to rage management as simply self-help would be to trivialize it. Rage is self-destruction at work. Managing rage brings peace; peace brings life. All that you value and work for in your life depends upon your learning to handle explosive anger.

Special Case: When Fear Boxes Us In

We learn from life's traumas. We learn what to avoid and what not to do. That's the beauty of our emergency memory and response system. That which we survive makes us wiser and more apt to survive again and again. Certain situations become associated with threat, and our fear responses keep us from going there. Sometimes, however, we learn too well.

One difficulty we can get into following trauma is when our fears become generalized. Not only do we avoid dangerous situations, but we also avoid similar situations even when they aren't dangerous. We lose the ability to distinguish between what does and what does not represent a threat. Our comfort zone closes in, and our ability to move about in the world becomes artificially restricted. We develop internally imposed "no-fly zones" that are enforced by panic.

> *Jeannie sat in her truck in the parking lot. Her therapist was next to her. It was all Jeannie could do to maintain control. She was visiting the site of her workplace trauma for the first time since the incident occurred. It had been nearly four months and she had been unable to return to work.*
>
> *She and her therapist had set the stage for this visit. They had worked hard at sorting through her memories and desensitizing what they could. Jeannie had spent much time learning how to raise and lower her arousal level at will. She had rehearsed the visit and had planned what to do if her feelings overwhelmed her. Now she was staring at the real thing.*
>
> *"I see an empty parking lot. What are you seeing?" the therapist asked.*
>
> *"The ball of fire. It was huge, bigger than anything. I'm hearing the gunshots."*
>
> *The therapist said, "It's hard when others can't see what you saw, or hear what you still hear." Jeannie looked at him. He continued, "You know, others have no idea what it was like for you. Why don't you try to breathe yourself down like we practiced?"*
>
> *Forty minutes later they were back in the truck. After using the calming and desensitizing techniques they had developed, Jeannie had been able to get out of the truck and walk through the site, reliving much of the incident as it had transpired. She still teetered*

on the brink of being upset and fearful, but she was able to function in a location where she had previously been unable to go.

They sat quietly, looking at the parking lot. "What do you see, Jeannie?" the therapist asked.

"The parking lot. It's empty."

"And the ball of fire? The gunshots?" he asked.

"They're there if I let them be. But right now it's empty." She smiled.

The next step would come in a couple of weeks when she was ready for it. They would arrange for the building to be opened on a Saturday so she could walk through the events that had taken place inside. Eventually, she would be able to return to work. More importantly, Jeannie was able to reclaim lost ground within herself.

Before doing this intensive work in therapy, Jeannie could not return to work even though the danger had passed. Her job—maybe even her career—was on the line. If she could not redefine the workplace as friendly territory, her life would become unduly limited.

Getting where we need to go and doing what we want to do are central to our self-esteem and our ability to live complete lives. When we are bound by trauma-based fear into restrictive patterns and limited options, it's time to take action. Pushing back these boundaries is possible.

Guidelines for Site Visits

The guidelines Jeannie followed for visiting the site of a traumatic event apply to any circumstance where you feel paralyzed by fear. The fear is an acute stress reaction to reminders of the traumatic incident. As you venture out to reclaim territory, understand that you must gradually learn to tolerate increased exposure to the reminders. Consider adapting the normal ASR management techniques to handle your fears. Below are the guidelines that Jeannie found useful. Remember that they can be applied any time you need to challenge your self-imposed boundaries.

— Plan the visit in advance. Decide what you want to accomplish. What sort of problems do you have with visiting the location? If you find yourself avoiding it, you are restricting your life options. One goal might be to be able to go there in the first place. Another might be to be comfortable once you are there. A third might be to "befriend" the place; after all, it is a significant place for you and a reminder of a situation you are trying to come to terms with. A fourth reason to go there might be to help you surface repressed memories you are trying to discover that are connected with the place.

— Familiarize yourself with the guidelines in Chapter 8 for managing acute stress response.

— Develop the ability to monitor your arousal level. In Chapter 8, we discussed what the various arousal levels feel like. It would be good to review that material again.

— Following the steps provided in Chapter 8, work out a plan for lowering your arousal level.

— Rehearse the visit, including practice in handling meltdowns. Ask yourself, "What will I do if I become upset?"

— Bring someone you trust into the plan. Tell the person what you want him or her to do to support you. Give the person specific actions to take, things to say, and reminders to give you in case you have trouble with overreactions.

— Take the visit one step at a time.

— Use breath, self-talk, imagery, and movement (see Chapter 8).

— Use your friend's support and suggestions.

— At each step, bring your arousal level back down to a manageable level.

— Back up or back off when you need to.

— When you get to the middle of the site, sit down and bring yourself to a state of being fully present.

— Walk around the location, looking at it from different perspectives.

— Use the phrase, "That was then, this is now." See the difference between then and now.

— Leave when you are ready.

— Talk about the experience with your friend. Write about it; draw it; tell others about it.

- If old—or new—feelings and memories come up, understand that they're normal.

- Afterward, celebrate your courage, daring, and accomplishment.

- Plan what to do next. Does another visit seem indicated? Do you wish to speak to a therapist about your visit? Is a journal entry called for, or can you imagine a ritual you would like to conduct to help you accomplish your visit goals?

Sometimes we cannot visit sites. For years Vietnam veterans wanted to return to Vietnam for personal healing; it wasn't until recently that the country was accessible. People who were abused as children often report wanting to visit the family home where the abuse occurred in order to try to gain perspective on their memories. They are disappointed to find the house torn down. In such cases, make-do substitutes can be used. Old war paraphernalia, photographs, and hand-drawn floor plans can suffice. The point is to spend time in the presence of reminders, reflecting on the internal feelings and images that arise so you can work on increasing your level of comfort.

Managing anger and fear opens up possibilities where there once seemed to be only limits. Another situation in which our arousal response places limits on our progress is when we experience such terrible loss that we cannot handle our own grief, because the feelings seem so unbearable.

Special Case: When Sadness Becomes Acute

Overwhelming events often involve loss. The loss of those we love is particularly difficult to accept in the best of times, and times of trauma are certainly not our best times. We can be left with feelings that are overwhelming and that frighten us by their intensity. In addition, our processing of those events interferes with our coming to accept our loss.

When my father died several years ago, I reverberated with mixed feelings. He had been a central fixture in my life while I was growing up and long into my adulthood. I went through days of disorientation and searching, longing and grieving. All of this was difficult in spite of the fact that I'd had years to prepare for his death. My father suffered from a cruel interplay between an arthritic condition that made every movement painful and advanced Parkinson's disease that caused constant shaking. By ten in the morning he would be drenched with sweat from the constant intense pain for which painkillers were largely ineffective. It was a living hell for him and for me. When his death finally came, it was a blessing and release. Even though I watched it come and prayed for its haste, even though we talked about it, planned for it, spent time reconciling differences and affirming our love, I wasn't ready. I was rocked. It has taken years to accept his loss.

Yet when my father-in-law died suddenly a few years later, it was an entirely different experience. His death came suddenly and prematurely. My family and his were shaken to their foundations. His loss was untimely and unacceptable. The whole family system and each of its members have been challenged by the powerful combination of the importance of the loss and the way in which it happened.

Sudden loss can be traumatic. Normal reactions to the loss are linked with the shocking sights, sounds, and feelings surrounding what happened and how the survivors were affected. The importance of the event is magnified by its circumstances. It's hard enough when the unthinkable must be thought and the unacceptable accepted. When traumatic images and reminders accompany the loss, the result can be levels of feeling that far exceed our capacity to cope.

When Loss Is Unbearable

When we grieve the loss of someone close—whether that loss is due to death, divorce, or the end of a relationship under other circumstances— we must savor that person's memory. Even if we wanted the divorce or separation, even if we recognize it ultimately as a positive thing in our life, in most cases we still must grieve the loss of what we once shared. We must also emotionally face the question, "Now what?" This is a process of reckoning, an emotional calculation and weighing of the consequences of life after loss. It is normal to experience waves of emptiness and to feel completely wretched. Our web of purpose and meaning has been ruptured. Grieving is the process of reweaving that web.

To do this, we revisit the place the person we lost occupied in our history. We replay our inner home movies and review the scrapbooks of our mind. We immerse ourselves in the reliving process in order to formulate the new issue confronting us: "If love causes this much pain, can I ever risk loving again?"

This is the normal grief process. It involves intense feelings. But when the memories or reminders trigger intense fear reactions and even a wholesale loss of control—hysteria—we can no longer grieve. We can no longer function, and we shut down. At the bottom of this is an inability to tolerate the intense feelings of loss. The wrenching ache caused by facing the reality of loss is unbearable. It literally blows our circuits.

The Key to Recovery: Tolerating Emotional Extremes

Trust that you need to feel your feelings. They are part of the normal process of accepting loss and moving on. No matter how badly you wish not to move on, when you are ready you will. But first you have to feel the feelings. When the feelings are running high, you need to find ways to tolerate them.

The principles of managing acute stress response are helpful here. If the feelings become so intense that you begin to become agitated or begin to shut down, use the strategies presented in Chapter 8 to keep you in the present.

The process is similar to working with fears. If you can gradually expose yourself to increased feeling and use the ASR strategies to keep your reactions within the functional range, you can stay with your feelings. Over time, you will be able to tolerate more extreme feeling. Eventually the feelings will work themselves out.

Give Feelings a Time and Place

The following ritual allows you to give your feelings a particular time and place to be expressed. It builds in a structure to assist you in managing the extreme feelings.

— Set aside a special place where you will not be disturbed.

— Set aside a specific time period, fairly short to begin with.

— Arrange to have someone to talk to after your session.

— Bring objects, pictures, or other reminders of your loved one.

— Bring appropriate music—one kind that is comforting and another that is evocative and connected with the person lost.

— Bring writing paper, pen, and drawing material.

— Set a timer. This limit provides security.

— Now, grieve. Without editing yourself or worrying about "looking silly," allow yourself to feel and express your intense emotions of loss and sadness. Cry, wail, gnash your teeth, holler into a pillow—whatever it takes.

— Use evocative music, pictures, and reminders to trigger your feelings.

— Use comforting music, writing, and drawing to help contain your feelings.

— Use acute stress response strategies (breathing, self-talk, movement) to keep your feelings manageable.

— When the timer rings, end your grieving session.

— Talk to your support person if you need or want to.

— Later, write about the experience. Plan for your next grieving session.

The more often you can do this, the more fluent you can become in allowing your feelings to work for you instead of against you. Eventually, you can use the same techniques to visit places that were important to your relationship with the lost person. This allows you to retake parts of the world and parts of your history that belong to you.

Opening to Peace

Armed with these strategies, you can work to break cycles of panic and rage that come between you and your loved ones. You can also identify when negative behaviors such as avoidance or substance abuse are based upon intolerable fear, grief, or anger responses, and move to redirect this energy constructively.

Letting go of underlying chronic fear, anger, and sadness takes time and effort, but doing so brings peace and opens the door to positive feelings of joy, excitement, and possibility. These positive feelings can be frightening at first, but you can learn ways to experience them that make your life richer, fuller, and more worthwhile.

THINGS TO THINK AND WRITE ABOUT

- Have you taken some time to inventory the contexts (times, places, and circumstances) that seem to trigger your problem feelings?

- Consider writing extensively about your attempts to manage strong and difficult emotional reactions.

- Have you investigated—alone or with assistance—the background and origins of your intense emotional reactions?

- Have you investigated the twelve-step program, Emotions Anonymous, designed for people whose lives are adversely impacted by overwhelming feelings?

- Might a professional be able to help you deal with difficult and overwhelming feelings?

CHAPTER 10

Dealing with Withdrawal, Numbing, and Depression

Ed Bilsie was a soft-spoken man, a trait that belied his accomplishments and his past. As executive director of one of the state's most powerful trade organizations, Ed made friends and had influence. The members he served were among the wealthiest and most well connected. His complaint? He really wasn't sure. His wife, another of my clients, had sent Ed for therapy.

We explored why she might have recommended therapy. He figured maybe it had to do with his not being happy and that maybe some of the passion had gone out of their marriage. "Are you happy?" I asked.

"Well, I don't know," he replied. "I'm not unhappy." He thought for a minute or two. "I'm not sure that matters a lot."

Death can come in different forms. Some forms work more slowly than others. One set of delayed stress symptoms gradually robs us of life. Dissociative reactions, withdrawal, and depression are due in part to brain-chemical imbalances, in part to being unable to cope, and in part to psychological issues. These underarousal reactions can be lethal in the long term.

One way that they are lethal is obvious: There is a higher risk of suicide among people who are depressed and dissociated. The other form of lethality is less obvious. When we are unable to respond positively to the world and those around us, we lose life on a daily basis. We become numbed to feeling, and we withdraw into ourselves. Little by little, we die to the world.

Calling in Air Strikes on Our Own Position

During military operations, ground troops being overrun by the enemy sometimes dig in, hunker down, and call for an air strike on their own position. By thus eliminating enemy soldiers who are more exposed, the "friendlies" who live through the bombing have a chance of surviving their otherwise certain death. Likewise, in the face of unbearable posttraumatic effects, when our mind simply cannot bear additional intense feeling, it "hunkers down"—it shuts down and waits for the storm to pass.

In Chapter 4, we talked about the difficulty of integrating dramatic memories into our map of the world and our place in that world. When the memories are linked with powerful feelings, our conscious mind struggles to keep them locked away. When that doesn't work, it shuts down. The result is temporary quiet purchased at a high price.

Withdrawal from living includes pulling away from those we love and the activities that make our lives worthwhile. Interest, involvement, and passion are blunted or even lost. We fade from the world into a self-protective psychological cocoon. Refusing to live fully, we partially die.

Brain Fade

The physiological effects of stress make coping difficult. As was pointed out in earlier chapters, after an overwhelming event the chemistry of the human brain literally works differently, for both the short term and the long term. Therefore, when we are suffering numbing and withdrawal, we feel different, act differently, and see the world differently. We experience the world as overwhelming. Our ability to understand and deal with the constant bombardment of problems, demands, and needs is impaired. We can't cope with our own reactions to the intensity of the world we experience. We need to take evasive action. Whether induced by chemical imbalance or the need for psychological protection, the mind sometimes shuts down in the face of overstimulation. We just fade out. It feels easier to deal with the agony of turmoil by just not feeling at all. This fading may take the form of social withdrawal, psychological dissociation, or depression.

Withdrawal

The term for avoiding demanding situations or people is *social with-*

drawal. Milder forms of withdrawal can include avoiding friends and family or becoming immersed in activities that keep you away from others. Withdrawal is about avoiding reminders of a painful event or of situations that make you think about the event. It may also be a way to avoid any situation that you find too stressful. In fact, you can eventually develop a tendency to withdraw as a general approach to all situations.

More serious forms of withdrawal can cause your life to change. Some people withdraw from life so much that they become reclusive, sever ties to others important to them, or even move to remote locations. Life has become unbearable, so they drop out of life as they knew it. How many good lives are lost to withdrawal? How many families are lost and dreams forgotten?

Dissociation

Ed Bilsie, whom we met at the beginning of the chapter, suffered from mild dissociation. Minor vexations affected him as they would most people. He got frustrated, irritated, worried, or a little upset. Larger annoyances, however, failed to elicit much more response than that. And when major insults, losses, or threats occurred, Ed still only grew frustrated, irritated, worried, or a little upset. It was as if his feeling gauge never reached much higher than the bottom.

This tied his wife into knots. Overdrawn bank accounts, the kids' new braces, news of impending storms—familial, political, international, or otherwise—simply did not raise Ed's blood pressure. She felt he either wasn't listening or didn't care. That—and their diminishing romance—is what drove her to drag him into therapy. Of course, he wasn't too upset at having to come.

What neither of them appreciated was that Ed cared as much as he could. But when caring became too intense, he automatically shut down. His wife's feelings of being abandoned were right on. Ed stayed detached, and as a result his wife did not feel wanted. The important fact for their relationship was that he couldn't feel, not that he wouldn't.

Dissociation means losing contact with your own feelings or even thoughts. Mild dissociation can mean staying uninvolved, not identifying with your own or others' worry, sadness, or anger. However frustrating this may be to other people, the person who is dissociating is in worse shape. Where life offers full servings of excitement, passion, involvement, love, sharing, thrills, meaning, and satisfaction, the person who is dissociated gets emotional oatmeal. Dissociation involves shutting down to life.

Depression

Depression takes a wide variety of forms as well, ranging from feelings of unhappiness and gloom to the development of bizarre thoughts and suicidal tendencies. Like dissociation, depression begins with withdrawal but develops its own particular brain chemistry and behavior pattern.

Most people go through periods of mild depression. Normal changes and life events can cause great sadness and periods of mourning. Any time we must let go of people, routines, or things we love, we have to regroup. That takes time. It's normal to feel bad while we develop new attachments.

Moderate depression is more serious. We may lose interest in things that used to provide us a sense of involvement and satisfaction. Our relationships can be affected and our work can suffer. We may enter periods of melancholy and withdraw into ourselves. Being affected by events in the world and within us isn't necessarily a bad thing. It is a sign that we have the capacity for great feeling and great concern. Someone once said that you can't trust someone who can't manage a good depression now and then; it's a sign of character. There's probably a bit of truth in that.

Serious depression must be taken very seriously indeed. We will examine it a bit later in this chapter.

Where Has Life Gone?

What's at stake in each of these ways of becoming unresponsive to the world is the loss of joy and satisfaction in living. Going inward is an important part of life, but taken too far, it robs you of life itself. It is suicide by degree. It also becomes habit-forming.

Withdrawal in the face of stress is normal. But just as rage, hysteria, or panic during normal times is neither normal nor healthy, dissociation and depression are not either. The good news is that shutdown to normal life stressors can be managed. The same techniques that you use to manage acute stress response can be used to counteract shutdown.

Analyzing your personal patterns of withdrawal, dissociation, and depression can help you to understand how they simultaneously protect and destroy.

What Can We Do?

To intervene in the pattern of shutdown reactions you have to understand their downward spiral. To help you gain insight into your patterns, write down your answers to the following questions. Over the next few weeks, continue to reflect on these questions and to observe yourself with them in mind. Write about any new insights you gain.

First, instead of focusing on how miserable you feel or how everything is overwhelming, begin by determining *where* and *when* your shutdown reactions occur. What is the context? What are the triggering conditions? Sometimes you can take action before your reactions take hold. If you can stabilize the situation, you won't need to shut down.

Another question to ask yourself is whether there are signs of an impending shutdown. You have lived with your reactions for a long time. Are there subtle or not-so-subtle thoughts or feelings you have before shutting down? If so, you can take countermeasures in the early stages of withdrawal before you attempt escape or slide into dissociation or depression.

Look at the nature of your shutdown cycle. How do you interpret the situation? What are your feelings or body reactions? How do you describe them to yourself or others? Can you shift your thoughts in order to shift your feelings? Can you coach yourself in how to handle your physical and mental reactions, or even in how to handle the situation itself? Steps for changing how you talk to yourself and how you think about a situation are listed in Chapter 8.

Can you kick your body into gear? Steps to do so are also outlined in Chapter 8. Advance planning is the best way, but the plans must be followed even if they seem like they won't work. A good operating rule with shutdown is to act as if you *can* pull out of it, i.e., "Fake it till you make it!"

Countermeasures for Episodes of Emotional Shutdown

Chapter 8 offered strategies for handling shutdown in the face of overwhelming incidents. Goals designed to break the cycle of decline include

- refocusing your attention outward

- shifting your thoughts (and, hence, expectations) about the incident

- attending to the present
- raising oxygen levels
- initiating the arousal response
- increasing your activity level
- turning passivity into productive activity

Troublesome episodes of withdrawal, dissociation, and depression can be looked at as emergency responses to reminders, situations, or conditions you experience as overwhelming. You can follow the above goals to plan for managing temporary episodes of recurrent postincident shutdown. However, each part of your plan must be flexible and appropriate to the stage of the reaction. In other words, it's better to employ countermeasures at each step in the cycle to redirect your reaction back toward normalcy. The table on page 161 gives a range of actions you can take to achieve the objectives listed above. They are arranged to follow the progression from thoughts to feelings to body processes to behavior, as described in Chapter 8. For more explanation of how to use these techniques, review the section in Chapter 8 titled "What to Do: Tools for Managing ASR" or consult the Emergency Guide at the front of this book.

Incorporate these countermeasures into your planning. When you find yourself fading, use them. Don't expect immediate turnaround. Learn from each episode and fine-tune your plan. Most importantly, don't give up! It takes a while—sometimes a long while—to relearn how to manage reactions that have gone out of control. Be patient and be persistent. Reclaiming your life is worth it!

There are times, however, when things become serious enough that taking action is more than just a matter of making life better. Serious forms of dissociation and depression can become life threatening.

Serious Forms of Dissociation and Depression

Serious forms of dissociation can include becoming so out of touch with yourself as to be unable to feel anything at all, having thoughts you experience as belonging to someone else, hearing voices, or even developing other personalities. Pathological levels of dissociation cost us our sanity.

Depression could be described as evasive action in the face of too much bad news. But when evasive action becomes pathological, it is a dif-

TOOLS FOR RESPONDING TO EMOTIONAL SHUTDOWN	
Tool	*How to use it*
Focus	Use positive, empowering self-talk; speak to others about how they perceive the situation
Thoughts and expectations	Visualize positive actions and successful outcomes
Attend to the present	Ignore memories and imagination; focus on the present
Oxygen	Initiate quick breaths; stretch your body
Arousal	Get up and get moving; shake it off
Activity	Take a power walk; exercise; do a ritual
Direction	Find something useful to do; find support and assistance

ferent story. Clinical depression marks the transition from unhappiness to illness. Serious depression can kill you.

Managing shutdown means knowing when to stand and fight and when to call for reinforcements. When dissociation and depression reach certain levels, it's time for help.

When Dissociation Becomes Toxic

Clinical forms of dissociation require more than a wake-up call, motivational seminar, or inspirational reading. Even those who treat PTSD realize that dissociative disorders require special approaches to standard treatment. Certain signs indicate when dissociation has reached the stage at which self-help is too little help.

The following are signs that it is time to get professional assistance:

- You feel trapped within yourself or uncomfortably cocooned from the world.

- You are experiencing troubling lapses of memory.

- You hear voices in your own head, or you hear voices when no one is around.

- You have distressing feelings that are unexplainable.

- Your body is plagued with unexplainable sensations or reactions.

- Some of your thoughts do not seem to belong.

- People you trust are telling you about things you have done that you do not remember.

- You find yourself shifting between dramatically different sets of thoughts and feelings.

- You do things sometimes that you don't remember later or that you usually would not do.

If these things are happening, or if others are telling you that they are happening, you definitely need to talk to a professional. These are signs that something is wrong that you can't fix by yourself. Do yourself and your family a big favor by taking these signs seriously and acting on them.

Taking Depression Seriously

What clinical depression looks like and what it feels like are two very different things. From the outside, a clinically depressed person usually looks quite wooden, although sometimes he may go through periods of manic agitation. Inside, however, there is great chaos. The pond that outwardly appears to be still is churning beneath the surface.

What Clinical Depression Looks Like

My client Tom was clinically depressed. A sometime weightlifter, Tom was large and tended to put on weight. He went through long periods of unemployment and, consequently, self-recrimination about not having achieved what he thought he should have. Outwardly Tom looked like most people most of the time, although maybe a little more quiet or subdued. Every now and then, however, he began to spiral downward. Usually something triggered his depressive episode. He first became sullen and withdrawn; then as days passed he went blank. If you asked Tom questions about his feelings or confronted him with his behavior, his face darkened to the point where you could hardly recognize him. His features thickened and became heavy. Suicide invariably came to Tom's mind as a possible avenue of escape.

What Clinical Depression Feels Like

In *Darkness Visible*, award-winning writer William Styron's courageous and moving account of his own depression, he struggles to put words to his experience. Styron describes the intense loneliness, the irrational behavior, and the strong feelings that are caused by depression. His episodes of darkness were terrible. Although he appeared blank and immobile, he was enduring "mind-storms," thunderous waves of rumination and emotion that left him paralyzed and unable to act. Depression is not dissociation. It is torture.

When you are depressed you feel as if you suffer from a terminal social disease. The first casualty is your belief in yourself. It is humiliating to feel so inadequate and out of control. You know you are letting down those around you. There seems to be no way anyone could possibly understand what you are going through. You are afraid you will die and terrified that you might not. For Styron to come out publicly with his eighty-four-page self-disclosure was a brave act of outreach to others who might also feel isolated in their suffering. A friend of mine who suffers periodic bouts of depression handed me Styron's book. Look, he was saying to me, this is how it is!

This swamp of feeling is sometimes punctuated by a periodic extreme release of energy. Some sufferers of depression, like Tom, are hit by moments of extreme high. Their feelings turn to wild exuberance, optimism, and frantic behavior. These episodes usually don't last long and are often followed by a crashing return into the dark.

When Depression Is Too Dangerous to Ignore

Whereas withdrawal and dissociation keep you from living, depression can kill you. When life feels overwhelming and intolerable, suicide can seem like the only way out. Suicide is a seductive but permanent solution to a temporary problem. It's like cutting off your foot when you stub your toe. Even if you can't find any reason to live, don't do this to those you love. If you find yourself entertaining thoughts of beaming up out of this life because you can't bear it here any longer, get up and get help now. With help, you can ride out the storm.

The following are signs that the problem is bigger than you are. They are the trouble lights on your dashboard that tell you that you are in deep trouble and in need of outside help. Find help immediately if

- you can't bear the clamor inside your own head
- your depression is driving your family away
- you are missing work, or people are telling you that your work is suffering
- you are losing sleep to the point of exhaustion
- suicide seems like the only way out

Clinical depression and dissociation can be managed. They require professional assistance, however. Many folks feel it is a mark of failure on their part to resort to counselors and doctors. They believe they should be able to take care of their own business. If that is how you feel, you might consider what you learned during the experiences that started this condition in the first place: The world is bigger than you. Events can crush us. It's just a plain, simple fact that none of us can leap tall buildings at a single bound and stop racing locomotives. We cannot single-handedly make terror threats go away, bring political or economic firestorms under control, or change global events. We are limited—every one of us. Part of our strength as human beings lies in knowing when to ask others for help. Do it and live. Live—and then return the favor to others.

Surfacing: The Larger Journey Back

The strategies presented in this chapter can give you an edge in heading off episodes of depression and dissociation. By weaving strategies into intelligent defense planning, you can anticipate personal crashes and take action to stay focused and functioning. This will allow you the room to put a larger plan into effect. Once you can maneuver around unmanageable extremes, you will be in a position to begin turning back on to life. You have been languishing in the deep waters of personal reconstruction. Your journey toward recovery requires that you resurface.

> *Ed didn't seem to really want to be in therapy. On the other hand, there wasn't much else he wanted to be doing, and it was good to keep his wife off his back. I offered him a way out. He did mention that he wanted to read. I suggested that maybe we could just meet once a week and talk about things we were reading. He brightened. I'm not sure what he was expecting in therapy but it wasn't this. We*

started through the W.E.B. Griffin series of novels set in World War II. And we talked.

After a number of months—and a number of novels and wide-ranging conversations—Ed came in with an announcement. The other day he had been driving home from work along his normal route. The road wound through some hills near a lake and past a small rural airport. A faded billboard read, "Flying Lessons: Inquire Within." Ed had seen this billboard for years. It had a picture of a small single-engine airplane banking through some clouds. Whenever he saw the billboard, he wondered what it would be like to fly. This time was different. He slowed to make the turn into the drive leading to the airport. It was time to inquire within.

Hidden Agendas: Uncovering Our Attachments to the Past

Part of the larger plan for moving beyond habitual withdrawal, dissociation, and depression involves rooting out ways in which we hang on to the past. In the film *Sophie's Choice* (based on another of William Styron's books), Sophie lives a life of postwar melancholy in New York City. During the war, when she lived in Europe, she and her two children were being shipped to a concentration camp. A sadistic guard forced her to choose one child to save; if she didn't, both would be killed. She was haunted by the choice. The torture devised by the guard was ingenious; seeds of self-hatred were sown that brought more pain than any beatings, humiliation, or death ever could. By her choice, she was party to her child's death. Understandably, this was a part of her past she had trouble letting go of. The film is about her making the decision whether or not to live. Her guilt over a past action kept Sophie, just as it does many of us, from allowing herself to feel joy and fulfillment in the present.

A FORMULA FOR NOT-LIVING	
Recurring thoughts	*Resulting belief*
I did what I shouldn't have done	I don't deserve joy
or... I didn't do what I should have done	pleasure, or
or... I survived when others didn't	satisfaction

Another way of living in the past is by staying attached to bygone moments of glory. Our worst times are often our most memorable times. During disasters or war, for instance, we witness other people performing selfless acts of bravery or self-sacrifice. Sometimes, during the heat of the moment, we do more and better than we ever expected. Despite the awful memories and suffering, we recall those times as moments of direction. During an extended crisis, life can take on a special glow of purpose and meaning unparalleled during normal times. We may develop a confusing nostalgia or longing for that time of struggle when bad was mixed with good.

Preserving the Past by Refusing to Live

Glory quickly fades. The importance of past moments and recognition of past deeds get eclipsed by the latest news, trends, fashions, and concerns. Those whose lives were affected or even defined by events in the past often find themselves struggling with impulses to bury the painful memories, but also to enshrine them. Symptoms are born of such inner conflict.

Ed Bilsie struggled with guilt. As we delved more deeply into his background, Ed revealed that he was a Vietnam veteran, having served as an infantryman with the Marine Corps. Ed had been in some of the most serious fighting in the war, in A Shau Valley and Khe Shan. At one point in our work together, he began writing a book about his experiences. He was a good writer, and his story recounted pitched battles and desperate moments. More importantly, from my point of view, a recurring theme emerged. Ed Bilsie— "Killer" to his combat buddies—had been horrified and transfixed by the consequences of his actions. His accounts of enemy contact juxtaposed the fear caused by unfolding situations with the numbing realization of the devastation caused by his return fire. He was alternately proud of his abilities in the field and appalled by what he had done. On the one hand, he longed to relive the intensity of combat and recapture the clear sense of brotherhood and purpose he felt as a nineteen-year-old for whom battle was a defining moment. On the other hand, he was haunted by memories of brutality and of the lives he had interrupted. He felt it was a fluke that he had been allowed to live while others, more capable and honorable than he, had not come home. By writing his book, Ed hoped that some of this

history and the stories of the men who had made it—who they were
and what they had gone through—would not pass unnoticed.

Ed is a middle-aged executive whose life seemed to have fallen into a more or less meaningless succession of days. He had a gnawing sense that he should have been doing something that warranted his being allowed to survive.

Like all of us, Ed was a collection of contradictions. He had very mixed feelings about his involvement in combat. On the one hand, in the dust and mud of Vietnam he had discovered an acceptance and sense of belonging he had never experienced before. On the other hand, that acceptance depended upon his abandoning many of his core values. Like many veterans, he couldn't believe what he had done there. Ed had both found himself and lost himself in the province of Quang Tri. Now, thirty years later, he moved through life as if half asleep, stirring only during certain gray days when he stood looking out the window, listening to raindrops falling on the large leaves of the bird of paradise planted outside his family-room window.

Keeping the Past Alive

A particularly perverse streak in human nature is our tendency to hold on to the outmoded, now useless sentimental reminders of what we have done and where we have been. Like most other things, this soft spot in our hearts for our history carries both good news and bad. The good is that we collect pictures, documents, and objects that tie us to our past and pave a sense of continuity into our future. This forges the identity that leads to integrity and direction. The bad news is that our lives can become cluttered with useless paraphernalia that confounds our effectiveness and impedes our growth. If we can't find things we need because they are hidden under piles of unneeded stuff, our decks are not cleared for action. We become mired in our heap of artifacts.

So it is with our emotional life. If our attachments to things of the past are compounded by the push and pull of mixed feelings and motives, we can hardly open up to the present moment or the future. If we hold on to the pain of the past in order to preserve the importance of those past moments—and if that in turn makes us crazy—we block our attempts to live fully. Many people struggling with the aftermath of crisis find that they are unable to move past the paralysis their symptoms create until they are able to transform the importance of the difficult events from their past into actions in the present. The story below illustrates how one person did just that.

Finding New Meaning in Old Distress

Sue Lee had been abducted at gunpoint and raped repeatedly for four hours in her car. Her recovery was slow but she persevered. After working through the experience in therapy she had gained the ability to keep her cool when confronted with reminders. She was unable to stay involved in intimate relationships beyond a certain point, how-ever. At the point at which deepening the relationship required trust, she would shut down. An important step for Sue occurred when she volunteered for Project Sister, a program that supports women who have been victimized by violence. Sue was in training to be able to accompany victims through their police-reporting and medical-exam procedures. The most difficult training session for her involved being in the room at the hospital where medical exams took place. She handled it well until she was leaving. As she prepared to pull out of her parking space, she put her car in drive instead of in reverse, and the car lurched over a concrete parking divider. Nothing was dam-aged. But as Sue acknowledged later, laughing nervously, "I suppose the training session bothered me more than I thought."

It may have been an unsettling experience, but by working with Project Sister, Sue is taking constructive action against a situation that has defeated her before. Through her repeated but controlled exposure to other violence victims, Sue could gradually gain the strength and even a sense of personal, enforceable boundaries that will allow her to become closer to others. In addition, Sue's ability to relate to rape victims will be enhanced by her own insight and experience.

Henri Nouen is a world-famous theologian. Late in life, he surprised his colleagues by taking a humble position as chaplain in a residential school for the mentally retarded. He continued to write about issues of faith, and one of his books addressed the issue of personal vulnerability among those who would help others. He said something in that book that stayed with me. In talking about the relationship between the ability to heal others and one's own hurt, he wrote, "It is not *in spite* of our woundedness that we are able to heal. Nor is it *because* of it. Rather, it is *through* our woundedness that we are able to heal." Healers do not need to be wounded to be able to heal, but they can use that experience to further their healing of others.

You don't have to be a healer to put your difficult life experiences to important use. Our backgrounds—however painful—open doors for us that would otherwise remain closed. Recovery is more than trying to get back to where you were before a bad incident happened. You may pine for the past, but you can never re-create it. In your recovery from difficult experiences, you gained new insights, priorities, and direction. You gained new skills and discipline. No matter how painful the experience was, you can be guided and enriched by it. The point is to use the suffering you have already endured as a pivotal point in deepening your life. If you can translate your past into a new, more informed view of the world—and a richer, more appreciative view of yourself—you can transform your pain into meaning and your meaning into direction.

Opening to Joy

In working with Ed Bilsie, I was amazed at how the effects of his reading and writing spilled out into the rest of his life. His wife began noting that Ed was taking more interest in things going on around the house, then more interest in her. She reported more squabbles with him, and I suggested that might be a good thing. He became more concerned with political rumblings within his organization and reported that he had delivered a pretty good speech at the annual meeting of the board of directors.

I liked to think it was the excellent therapy he was getting, but I kept thinking about those flying lessons. Can a metaphor sometimes become a new life? Ed's leaving the ground was not just about his flying away from memories or complications. Nor could I write off Ed's flying lessons as just a hobby. I remember the light I saw in his eyes during our session following his first cross-country solo.

Ed finished writing his book. It hasn't been published yet and maybe it is not destined to be. That remains to be seen. It brings satisfaction and completion to Ed, however, and an emerging sense of direction. At one point in our discussions, I became interested in Ed's background in history. Because Ed held a B.A. degree and no advanced degrees, he felt that his major in history had simply been a useful background for political activity. But he had loved studying it. Now military history, in particular, held Ed's fascination. "You know," I suggested, "you don't have to be a college professor to study history and to write and publish in the field. I could imagine you, with your interests and ability to organize folks, pulling together a network of others interested in a particular area like, say, World War II. Your group could share your work back and forth, maybe even do an electronic journal of your own."

Behind this suggestion was the thought that Ed needed to honor his own past. Whatever its downside, it was his personal history. Ed's active involvement with others' similar histories not only could provide an exoneration and reconciliation with that lost part of himself but also could open up a new focus of interest and passion. Instead of holding back for fear of unworthiness or of letting go of that which cannot be held, he could move forward toward self-acceptance and discovery.

THINGS TO THINK AND WRITE ABOUT

- Have you tried taking some time to identify the times, places, and circumstances that seem to trigger your feelings of being disconnected or depressed?

- Consider writing extensively about your attempts to manage these emotional reactions.

- Have you investigated—alone or with assistance—the background and origins of your fading and shutdown reactions?

- Are you able to discuss your reactions with people you trust?

- Might a professional be able to help you deal with bouts of depression and disconnection?

CHAPTER 11

Stabilizing Our Children and Families

This chapter explores ways to address the particular difficulties of parenting and fighting that undermine the stability of families during prolonged emergencies or following upset.

Children need continuity and security. If you are plagued with anger, panic, or overwhelming loss, your parenting can suffer. You probably have difficulty—more than you realize, perhaps—providing your child with a sense of stability and predictability. If you go through periods of fading or depression, you are likely to be distracted and absent from your child. With either or both scenarios, your child loses the continuity and security he or she needs. And you lose that special connection with your child that can provide you with a sense of belonging and "fit." Further, you may not feel so good about yourself as a parent.

Parenting During Difficult Times

When your feelings are in turmoil, you need time for yourself. Lean on others to help with the kids while you take the time you need. It is better to use parenting time positively for shorter periods than negatively for longer periods. The idea of "quality time" remains relevant. It doesn't mean going to fancy places or spending lots of money. It simply means remaining present when you are with your child and focusing upon what you are doing together. Instead of going to places like amusement parks or movies, try taking a walk together, attending a class function, or working together on a project.

Working with the other adults in your child's life is extremely important. Whether you are a single parent or part of a couple, you need to

coordinate your approach with them. It is critical that you work constructively with them through difficult parenting times. Parents are never off
duty, even if someone else is physically present with the child. During
postcrisis periods of self-examination and vulnerability, parents must continue to make parental decisions, set and enforce family rules, and provide
the warmth, security, and support their children need. Times of self-
doubt, intense feelings, and changing standards are precisely when your
children need you the most.

Security and trust issues are the most important with younger children. Pay particular attention to the child's feelings of safety. Remember
that—*from the child's point of view*—it isn't so much whether the child *is*
safe as whether he or she *feels* safe. Once you make them safe, concentrate
on making them feel that way.

With older children, safety is still an issue, but they also need to feel a
sense of continuity and of usefulness. Giving them productive roles in the
ongoing drama goes a long way toward reestablishing feelings of self-worth
and control.

Talking to Children after a Crisis:
An Example

Earlier in the guide we discussed guidelines for talking to kids in times of
uncertainty and increased anxiety. But what do we say to our children in
the aftermath of an actual crisis or disturbing event? And when do we
broach the topic with them? It's often hard to know the answers to these
questions. Sometimes we are afraid we will make a situation worse by talking about it. Other times we can hardly bear to deal with the matter ourselves. We may be overwhelmed by our own feelings, or we may simply be
at a loss about what to say. However, it is more important to talk to children in a way that shows them we care than it is to know "just the right
thing" to say. To illustrate the principles of effective conversations with
children, we will follow one family dealing with a crisis.

> *Fifteen-year-old Katie Smith, in tears, approached her parents one
> evening and told them she'd heard something awful about Justin, her
> eighteen-year-old brother. A classmate told her that Justin had been
> present the weekend before when another kid had nearly died from
> an accidental heroin overdose. According to the classmate, Justin*

had been alone with the young man at his house when the guy had OD'd. Then, apparently, Justin called 9-1-1, hid in the bushes to make sure the paramedics arrived, and then slipped away before anybody saw him. A week later, Justin's friend was still in the ICU. Nobody was accusing Justin of using drugs himself, Katie assured her parents, but still, how terrible he must feel to have been mixed up in the situation at all. When Katie had asked Justin about it, he'd gotten furious and yelled at her to mind her own business. She was clearly upset about feeling that she had to come to her parents, because she didn't want to seem like a tattler. But she didn't know what else to do.

Hearing this story, Katie and Justin's parents, Rob and Karen, were upset. But they thanked Katie for telling them. They reassured her that she had done the right thing by telling them, and they told her they would have to think about what to do. They also told her that she hadn't gotten her brother into trouble. Later, by themselves, they decided that Rob should approach Justin first.

How do you go about talking to an adolescent who clearly doesn't want to talk? The following strategies have been proven helpful in talking to children after crises. Some of them overlap with the guidelines given above for talking to kids about generalized fear and uncertainty. Here is how the Smith family used the recommended approach to help family members come to terms with a possible crisis:

1. Find a private space

If possible, find a comfortable, safe place to talk. Parents should talk to their children within the privacy of the family, and sometimes without other siblings present.

Rob knocked on Justin's bedroom door that evening before dinner. In a calm and kind voice, Rob told Justin he'd heard the rumor about what had happened. He told Justin he thought it would be a good idea to talk about it. He asked if now would be a good time. Justin was incensed. He shouted, "I can't believe she told you! And, no, I don't want to talk about it!"

2. Stay calm

In all probability, the child is experiencing uncertainty and self-doubt. Children look to parents to determine whether or not to be afraid. Your calmness tells the child that the situation can be talked about and that whatever she talks about will be accepted. Calming yourself may require taking specific steps such as those outlined earlier in the guide involving your mental, emotional, and physical processes.

> *Rob paused and took a deep breath. He knew better than to blow up or to beg Justin to talk just then. "Okay," he said. "Let's talk after dinner." Rob didn't force Justin to agree to talk, but instead went back and spoke with Karen about his own fears for Justin's well-being.*

3. Be honest with yourself

Keep in touch with your own feelings about and reactions to the child, the issues, and the situation. Self-awareness helps keep communication clear. If you feel you cannot handle the situation, ask someone else to help.

> *Rob was concerned. He really didn't think Justin used drugs, but he also knew better than to assume anything yet. He knew that Justin was beating himself up for not staying by his friend's side. After much conversation with Karen, Rob realized that he had been through something like this during his own adolescence, and that things hadn't worked out then. He had to be careful not to push Justin too hard. In this case, he decided an indirect approach would probably work best.*

4. Speak at the child's level

Use words, concepts, and gestures that the child can understand. Check for understanding as you go along. Don't provide information that might confuse or scare the child, and don't overload the conversation with more than the child needs to know.

> *After dinner Rob helped Justin with drying dishes. He told Justin the story of his own experience in college and how concerned he had been for another student's safety. Someone in his dorm had been drinking and had later attempted suicide. Rob was still mad at himself for not acting at the time and for not finding out for himself later how his friend had turned out.*

5. Read between the lines

Watch the child's behavior and reactions during the talk. Look for signs of fear or agitation. Check for attention span. Be aware of subtle messages.

Think about what these signs might mean. If you think you might be seeing something worth noting, inquire further; what you see may guide you to the most central issues your child is facing.

> *When Rob finished his story, he noticed that Justin had stopped washing dishes and was watching him. "Is that what you are worried about?" Rob asked gently. Justin looked away, wiping his hands repeatedly with the dishcloth.*

6. Validate the child's feelings
Feelings are neither right nor wrong. Whatever feelings the child is expressing, validate them. Often, lots of feelings clamor for expression; help the child to clarify them, and you will both watch the feelings change. Try putting words to a feeling, and asking whether they fit. If they don't, try others. Help the young person find the right words.

> *"Is that it, son?" Justin nodded. "I should have helped him out. I should have stayed there and answered questions for the paramedics, but I couldn't. I was afraid I'd get busted."*

7. Listen well
Good listening involves several skills. Use gentle, probing questions and comments to encourage clarification and elaboration. Maintain good eye contact. Use increasingly focused questions when appropriate (particularly when you suspect that something happened that hurt your child or someone else). Trust your hunches and check them out.

> *Rob asked Justin several questions—not so much to find out what happened, but rather to help Justin keep talking. "What have you heard about your friend?" he wondered.*

8. Show that you believe the child
Your job at this point is to listen and to facilitate expression. You are not a judge, jury, or investigator. Show confidence, trust, and faith that what the child is saying is the truth as he or she believes it to be.

> *Justin told his father he had arrived at his friend's house after the friend had shot up. The friend seemed "spaced out" and then collapsed. Seeing the paraphernalia, Justin realized what had happened and called 9-1-1. At the last minute, hearing the sirens approaching, he lost his nerve and fled. Rob listened intently, nodding at the*

appropriate moments and saying "Sure" and "Of course" at the
moments when he sensed Justin faltering.

9. Dispel fault

If the child was victimized, let him know that the incident was not his
fault. Be proactive about this, because victims tend to distrust and blame
themselves.

> *"Justin," Rob began, "I'm so happy that you handled the situation*
> *so well. A lot of guys would have just panicked and taken off. But*
> *you had the presence of mind to call 9-1-1. You may have saved his*
> *life. Son, I'm so proud of you! I can also understand your not want-*
> *ing to hang around for fear of being implicated, or maybe of having*
> *to testify against your friend. But you waited to see that the medics*
> *got there."*

10. Explore fears

Children often can talk about what happened to them, but may be unable
to express assumptions, questions, or fears they have about the incident.
By facilitating the expression of these assumptions, questions, and fears at
this point, you can empower the young person to deal with them.

> *"Tell me this," Rob asked, sensing that more was unsaid. "What*
> *have you heard about your friend's condition now?" Justin shrugged*
> *his shoulders, looking miserable. "What are you afraid of?" Rob*
> *probed further.*
>
> *Justin was quiet. "I dunno. I guess I'm mostly afraid that the*
> *damage is permanent. I want to know if he's really okay."*

11. Provide information

The right information at the right time can be very helpful. If you know
something about the incident, normal reactions to that kind of incident,
or actions that could be taken, consider sharing that information. Be sure
not to preach, however, and be sure that your own need to "do something"
is not clouding your judgment regarding the timeliness of the information.

> *Rob thought about the situation. "You know, a couple of things occur*
> *to me, Justin. One is that it is natural that you would feel this way. I*
> *can't feel just what you're feeling, but I imagine that some of it has*

*to do with your not knowing how he is. Maybe we could find out.
How could we do that?"*

*Justin thought for a minute. "Maybe they would know at the
hospital. I don't really want to call his family."*

12. Walk through the process

Children want to know what's going to happen next. When the time is
right, sharing what you know about certain processes can assist the child
in predicting and planning.

*"I doubt if the hospital would tell us anything," Rob said. "They
have to keep medical information confidential. Only the family
could tell us. Maybe we could call the family together?" Justin
shrugged.*

13. Explore resources

As soon as possible, explore with older children what resources they have
available, and what their support system provides. Assist them in deciding
to whom, when, and how to reach out for that support.

*"The other thing I'm pretty sure of is that his folks probably feel
pretty alone right now, and they are probably grateful that someone
had the sense to call 9-1-1. Have you met your friend's folks?" Rob
asked. Justin nodded. "How about if I go over to their house with
you?" Justin visibly relaxed.*

What Not to Do

We want to care for those we love. It's partly an urge to protect and partly
a desire to make our kids strong in the event we can't be there to take care
of them. We feel a need to provide correction and guidance, so they can
learn to do things on their own. But the impulse to correct can be a problem after a crisis, when our children are vulnerable. It's best to leave object
lessons for less stressful times.

It is a myth that any interaction is preferable to no interaction following a crisis. After frightening events, children are likely to be highly
impressionable and emotionally vulnerable. Careless messages, heavy
judgments, and bad advice can leave a lasting impression. Such bad medicine can amount to retraumatization. The following types of interaction
should be *avoided* when talking with a child who has experienced a critical
incident:

Don't make false promises

Do not tell children things you are unsure of, or that are untrue. If you are unsure of something, tell them, "I'm not sure, but I will find out for you." Do not say, "Everything is going to be all right" unless you have some way of knowing that to be true.

Don't fall apart

It's all right to shed some tears in empathy, but when interacting with a child who's in a critical situation, it is essential to maintain emotional control. Don't fall apart or react with excessive emotion; doing so sends the message that you can't be trusted with difficult information. The child has enough to cope with; he or she does not need to be forced to take care of your emotional problems as well.

Don't pass judgment

Facial expressions, body language, inferences, and questions can communicate judgments. Even "Why did you take so long to come to me?" signals an implied judgment that can be more than a vulnerable young person can handle. Focus on the person, not on what's "right."

Don't become an inquisitor

Don't play detective, searching for information with which to hang the perpetrator. Such inquisition will only drive the child away or make things worse. Instead, assist the child in revealing what he or she feels is necessary. Work with that.

Don't preach

Leave your opinions for another time. Don't rant or blame, castigate or pontificate. Let the child be the center of focus.

The guidelines presented here and in the preceding section encourage communication and decision making. They help the young person turn a negative event into a learning experience and they foster long-term development. Sometimes in the process of helping our children cope with what we perceive to be the problem, however, we discover other dimensions to the situation we hadn't anticipated. Perhaps the child was traumatized by the incident—or by a preceding event that you hadn't realized was so serious. Or, perhaps the child was the victim of abuse of which you were not aware. The next section helps you identify direct and indirect signs of trauma and abuse, and gives suggestions about what you can do.

Stabilizing Teens

Teenagers create added difficulties. Parenting adolescents is rarely easy. Although they do not take the moment-by-moment care that younger children require, they present unique challenges. Teens are struggling with issues of autonomy, peer influence, and continued dependence upon you. They need you to provide leadership, continuity, and security, but they also need to grow away from you. This remains true during times of fear and uncertainty. The demands upon you as a parent are complicated and contradictory under the best of circumstances. Your struggle to recover from personal crisis is not the best of circumstances. You may become more needy, more uncertain, and less stable at the time when they need you to be most balanced. It can be terrifying for both of you.

Young people struggle with two needs that are in constant conflict. First, they need to grow into independence. That means they need to make their own decisions and live with the consequences. On the other hand—though they would never admit it—they are still children. They want to know that their parents care about them, protect them, and will provide guidelines and limits for their exploration. Walking this parental tightrope is difficult under the best of circumstances and nearly impossible when the parent is haunted by past events. The good news is that while adolescents are quick to criticize their parents' mistakes, they usually do recognize honesty. If you are sincerely trying to do right by them, they will see and appreciate that fact.

Job number one is to create a supportive relationship environment that allows your teens to experiment with the various styles, positions, roles, and "persons" they are trying on for size, without abandoning them with an "anything goes" attitude. This balance minimizes confrontation and encourages communication about the more important things on teens' minds. In deciding where and when to put your foot down, you really have to decide how important each issue is. It's good to ask yourself the old cliché question: "Is this really the bridge I'm ready to die on?" Having said that, some bridges definitely qualify.

Job number two follows right on the heels of job one. It is to understand that your children need to push against you in the process of growing up. They need you to set boundaries, and they will go looking for them if you don't set them. Boundary testing is a continual process in a family with teens. But don't confuse needing boundaries with wanting them. There's great security in the parental protective shield, but teens also feel a natural need to challenge those boundaries. If you can establish a listening relationship within a guiding structure, your teens will be more apt to talk to you when they really need to.

Following a major life upset, you are likely to fear for your children's well-being. You may experience an intense need to help your teenagers become as strong as possible so they can weather the same storms you have encountered. You may fret over their safety and try to help them become as prepared as possible to deal with adversity. However, this can translate for them into pressure for achievement.

At best, they will perceive you as nagging, at worst as demanding and repressive. Perceived pressure definitely can contribute to their feeling of being unworthy. Kids who feel they have to qualify for attention and love don't learn that they are valued for themselves. Feelings of being undervalued and of falling short of expectations create a sense of shame. A downward social spiral can be triggered. Teens who feel inadequate develop a sense of isolation, which leads to a search for someone who will like them. This search for acceptance, in turn, can ultimately lead to your teens associating with a peer group with whom you feel very uncomfortable. Pressure that lets your children know you care is fine. Pressure that leaves them feeling like failures is toxic.

Don't live in panic over the future. Respect your children for who they are. Share the joy of their search for identity. Don't get crazy if your child looks or acts extreme; take it as an invitation to see what's behind the behavior. Many of the kids who look the most at-risk are, in fact, simply exploring themselves. Get to know your teens and their friends. Find out what their music and role models are all about. Get lyrics to the songs they listen to, and find out what the music means to them. Give your teens as much trust as they show they can handle, and don't be afraid to yank their chain when necessary. By this I mean don't be afraid to enforce rules or to place limitations on your teens' behavior when it is appropriate to do so. Teenagers need to know that you are present in their lives and that you can still provide a protective barrier. If your children know that you are genuinely interested and trying to do a good job parenting—particularly when you admit your fears, foibles, and mistakes—you will get respect.

Parenting well becomes even harder when the parents are separated, new adults are entering the family picture, or circumstances have led to changes in our ability to parent alone and we must get help from outside the family. The term for such changes is 'Coparenting.'

Strategies for Coparenting

In general, consistency in rules, consequences, and reactions is a virtue. Maximum cooperation between parental partners is important. During periods of turmoil, tensions can become a problem between parents, nerves can fray, and parenting can suffer. The following suggestions may help you navigate through stormy coparenting seas:

— Sort out the issues you are grappling with personally, and list the specific ways in which these same issues arise in your parenting.

— Establish guidelines and priorities for your own behavior. Do this by reviewing the discussions on countermeasures in Chapters 8, 9, and 10. Be aware of key times and situations that are particularly difficult, and refer to your personal action plan during those moments of difficulty.

— If you have a parenting partner (whether you live together or not), use a tag-team approach. Develop a signal system to call for help whenever one of you is becoming overwhelmed and overreactive, or is withdrawing and becoming underreactive.

— Establish a feedback system with your partner to help you give and receive observations about your parenting. If your partner is unavailable, set up a similar communication system with people who are in the position to observe both your children and you with them. Teachers, extended family members, or friends could assist.

— If you think it might help, involve a family therapist to help monitor your efforts, enrich your family experiences, work through roadblocks, and resolve conflicts.

— Have a conference table set aside for negotiations and conflict resolution. Have separate rules and procedures for such conferences. If your relationship is explosive and self-control is difficult, use a therapist to help you set up a successful procedure for negotiation.

— Establish rules and consequences only when you and your parenting partner are calm, rational, and in control. Consistency is where the magic lies, and you can't set and enforce consistent guidelines when you are angry and desperate. Involve your children in developing rules as much as possible.

— Work at setting aside time and creating situations to reinforce positive relationships and to rebuild and restructure negative relationships.

These suggestions are powerful tools to restabilize families during tough times. They can transform fragmentation and despair between family members and reinforce relationships. Sometimes, however, patterns of conflict become so explosive and destructive that they seem impossible to turn around. If this has happened, consider a more serious approach to coming to grips with family chaos.

Austere Triage for Family Arguments

Mental-health professionals used to consider arguments in the home as a time to get to the bottom of misunderstandings and resolve differences. Some held to the maxim, "Don't let the sun set on hard feelings." We encouraged clients to use conflict to learn to work out differences that stood between them and their loved ones. Indeed, these are good words to live by. They reflect the goals of an intimate relationship and open the way for increased love and understanding.

But what do you do when small differences quickly escalate into major fights? How do you handle a loved one who is so exhausted by uncertainty and fear that resolving differences seems to be someone else's romantic fantasy? And how do you protect your children from becoming collateral damage in a domestic war on terror?

First, get some perspective, and then get some help. Understand that what you need most right now is peace of mind. Your home and family should be and can be a place of refuge in a world gone mad. If you and your loved ones cannot solve the problems dividing you, it is time to admit that the problems are bigger than all of you. Bookstores abound in resources for strengthening families. Professionals can help. The time and money you spend now could really benefit and even save your family in the long run.

I am finding in my practice right now that my client families need more than the usual assistance with communication and conflict resolution. They need the sort of emergency family first aid that can buy them time to make longer-term adjustments possible. When arguing and fighting become commonplace in your family, it's time for a new approach. Fights must be triaged—rapidly assessed to determine treatment—and the bleeding must be stopped.

First Aid for Family Chaos

Believe it or not, you can take control of the fighting in your family. It's easy for fights to start when nerves are frayed, and it's hard to stop them. It's even harder when they start suddenly and seem to be simply continuations of the fights that came before. Chronic fighting usually follows a pattern, however. It often has a predictable trigger and follows an equally predictable course. Understanding how most fights start and how they escalate beyond control provides the key to taking appropriate action.

To put that understanding into action, however, we must first begin by establishing a procedure that enables us to stop fights when they start. Then we can begin to look for underlying causes.

> *Sandra Rolf became aware that she and her husband Jim seemed to be fighting more than talking since the war started. Her fantasy had been that home would be a safe haven in a world at war. Now it seemed that there were more ambushes in their bedroom than there were overseas. They had both become so defensive that a false move on either side would erupt into a firefight even before they knew what had started it. After consulting with a counselor, Sandra approached Jim with a plan. "How about," she suggested, "we call for a cease-fire and a cooling-off period once we realize we are get-ting into it again? Then later, when we both have done a little thinking, we'll sit down and start over."*
>
> *Following her suggestions seemed to help somewhat, and Jim seemed interested in writing down some rules for engagement.*

Although they still got into arguments too often over things that weren't all that important, they gradually fine-tuned their system. Pretty soon they found themselves coaching their kids on how to disengage, regroup, and try again later. Sandra began to hope again.

The following are some steps to take to get a grip on the fighting in your family if it seems to be intensifying out of control:

First, consciously change your thinking about the conflict and the words you use to describe it, using the processes presented in Chapter 8. Begin with yourself. Analyze your pattern of interaction with the other person; specifically, look at how escalating events trigger your shifts from one frame of mind to another. How do those shifts result in your own personal internal narrative? How do you start seeing things differently and shifting your expectations? You may want to get help from a professional to think this through. Before talking to the other person who is involved in the conflict, get clear on what's going on in your own head.

Next, do some strategic planning with the other person. Sit down together during a moment of clarity. Try to analyze what kinds of situations or topics lead to out-of-control conflict. If you can discern a pattern, you can make better contingency plans. Work out an agreement to break the pattern. If this discussion keeps triggering the old pattern of conflict, try communicating at first through written notes. Doing this eliminates reactions to nonverbal messages and creates an interlude for reflection.

Determine what situations—times of day, circumstances, or topics— commonly produce rapidly escalating fights. Make an agreement to avoid interaction, if at all possible, during these times. Decide when to make decisions regarding "hot" topics; choose other times or places to make these decisions so that you can avoid difficult circumstances.

Agree that each of you has the right to terminate any discussion you feel is spinning out of control. Decide what words to use when exercising your right, and agree that if the other does likewise, you won't pursue the issue. But remember to determine when and where you will take up the issue again.

Have an exit strategy. Know what to do if the other person is unable to disengage from the conflict. This is an action you will have to initiate and carry out on your own. You may have to physically leave the situation.

Have a regrouping plan. Breaking away from an argument doesn't solve anything. It just keeps it from doing more damage. Once the intensity of the moment has subsided, the two parties involved in the conflict need to have a way to resume communication. If decisions must be made, follow the plans you have made for doing so. If not, you can focus upon reestablishing the bond between you. Many couples have preestablished meeting places and routines for regrouping.

Having a way to diffuse escalating arguments creates a basis for trust, so long as the parties involved in the conflict follow through and resolve outstanding issues. It also offers a further benefit. It lowers the conflict level in the home and makes it easier to rebuild a sense of sanctuary. Finally, children benefit. Attention can be diverted to helping them cope with the normal stresses of growing up and the additional worries of the times.

Rebuilding family trust is important; the family is where your heart lives. If you want to strengthen your family's resilience after upsets and rebuild your connection with them, there are two other parts of this book to explore, if you haven't already. Check out the Emergency Guide and the guide to Resources at the front of the book. They provide you with detailed steps to manage further crisis events. Once the chaos subsides, you will be in a position to rebuild your relationships. Chapter 13 also suggests ways to reconnect with those you love in a more satisfying and productive way.

THINGS TO THINK AND WRITE ABOUT

- How does your family get along lately?

- Do your children seem to reflect underlying tensions that might arise from insecurity or fears?

- What are some of the main situations that seem to trigger family upset?

- If there seems to be more fighting within your family, what have you tried to do to calm the discord? Is it working?

CHAPTER 12

Getting Professional Help

It's one thing to know you could benefit from professional help, another to know what kind of help to get, and still a third to know what to expect when you find this help. This chapter explores these issues. Because I am a practicing therapist, I have a particular view of therapy and how it can best be done. My approach may or may not be the most effective; it's just what seems to work best for my clients. For that reason, I will discuss therapy in this chapter from my own professional point of view.

Sometimes people ask me when they should see a therapist. I tell them they shouldn't see a therapist until they have suffered long enough. If they aren't ready to change, they won't. They tell me they have a brother-in-law who went to therapy and he isn't any better—as a matter of fact, he's worse now. I tell them I know three mechanics whose cars need work, three housecleaners whose homes are messy, and three therapists who are crazier than their brother-in-law. Therapy isn't an exact science and therapists aren't all the same. When they tell me they can't bear their circumstances any longer, I tell them maybe they could benefit from seeing a therapist.

Seeing a professional can really help, but you have to choose your therapist well. The first section of this chapter addresses frequently asked questions about therapy and therapists in general. After that, I discuss therapy for fear and anxiety, for family problems arising from emergencies, and for trauma. Next I outline a few therapeutic approaches I have found useful in my own practice. The chapter closes with some thoughts on finding a therapist who is right for you.

Frequently Asked Questions about Therapy

Certain questions about therapy come up time and time again. They cut to the nub of what therapy is and what to expect. They deal with misconceptions and illusions about therapy. Addressing these questions is an ideal place to start.

"What's the Point of Therapy?"

The point of therapy is to quit hurting. The point of therapy is to figure out what to do to make the pain go away. Maybe therapy won't work; maybe it will make you feel worse before you feel better. There are lots of *maybes*. Studies show that therapy works a lot of the time. Besides, it beats the alternative. If you are suffering, therapy might help.

There is another point to therapy; it is the same as the point to all of our life struggles. Making you feel better can be the start of a deeper process of personal growth. Through your work with a therapist, you may make significant progress toward becoming the person you have the potential to be. Much of the excitement I find in being a therapist lies in being a part of that process of discovery.

"How Do Therapists 'Do' Therapy?"

I can't speak for all therapists. Heavens, there must be fifty thousand of us in the United States alone. We come in all sizes, shapes, and specialties. We have different training, different areas of expertise, and different ability levels. Some of us are trained to work quickly, some longer. Our styles of working reflect our personalities as well as our training and background. And we all have limitations. We are just people doing a job. We are not judges, parent substitutes, punching bags, or demigods, even though our clients may want to give us that type of status. Some of us are more effective than others; all of us have shortcomings, biases, and vulnerabilities. Most of us are better with certain types of clients and problems. None of us works magic, although once in a while it feels like magic to our clients or their families. Sometimes we even surprise ourselves.

"How Long Will It Take?"

It used to be that therapy took a long time. Freud, the "Father of Psychotherapy," saw clients every day for seven years. I knew a therapist who had a sign in his waiting room that read

HOW LONG COUNSELING TAKES	
Normal problems of living	One month
Anxiety, depression, and relationship problems	Three months to one year
Personality overhaul	One year or more

He told me that clients sometimes asked if the sign was for real. The reason he hung the sign was to raise the issues of clients' purposes for coming and what sorts of expectations they had. It helped to clarify their task. The specific time frames were not accurate; in fact, the time it takes to accomplish different therapeutic goals varies quite a bit for many reasons. The point of the sign had to do with the nature of the expectations. The fact of the matter is that even though some approaches, therapists, and clients work more effectively than others, some kinds of problems are simply more deep-set than others. Sometimes it just takes a while.

Newer therapies boast faster recovery. Lots of evidence is coming in that supports these claims. One of the new group of therapies is referred to as "body approaches." Therapists who do bodywork claim to reduce symptoms fairly quickly, and their clinical evidence is impressive. But therapists who focus upon the integration of traumatic experiences into their clients' personalities and daily lives argue that just relieving symptoms isn't enough.

"How Much Does It Cost?"

It depends. If your health insurance covers psychotherapy, or if you qualify for treatment under various government-sponsored assistance programs, it might not cost much at all.

If you opt for private care, it can be expensive. Generally speaking, family therapists and licensed clinical social workers cost less than clinical psychologists, and all of them cost less than psychiatrists. Further, it's not so much what license they hold as it is their training and effectiveness. It's best to ask around for recommendations. Also keep in mind that some regions are more expensive than others: A private therapist in Winslow, Arizona, is probably going to charge a great deal less than one on the West Side of Los Angeles or the Upper East Side of Manhattan.

It might be helpful to remember that the costs of psychological distress include discomfort, impact upon your job or career, relationship and parenting problems, and the loss of hope and joy. By not seeking therapy, you may be draining your life in these areas. Put another way, how much is it costing you to save money?

"What Happens in Therapy?"

Therapy has changed quite a bit since I was trained. It used to be that some therapists were careful to observe the slightest behaviors of their clients. They'd check out the way the clients' eyes darted around the room, the way they sat, and the chair they chose. If the clients chose the biggest or most central chair in the room, it was thought to be significant. If they glanced at their watch, it meant they didn't want to be there. If they got upset when the therapist drilled them too quickly with probing questions, they were thought to be resisting therapy. Going to therapy felt like a trip to the dentist or a tax audit. No wonder lots of appointments were conveniently forgotten!

There are now many different approaches to therapy. How the therapist acts, what he or she says or does, and what is expected of the client vary with the approaches. The therapist's own personal style and personality vary a lot as well.

It might help to begin with a closer look at one therapist whom I know fairly well. Me. Showing what things look like from my point of view might make it clearer from yours.

From My Side of the Room

Although I keep up on the professional literature, attend professional conferences, train others, and talk a lot to my colleagues, I don't really know what goes on behind the closed office doors of other practitioners. I can only speak for my own practice and draw a few generalizations about the practices of others. I like to think I'm pretty good at what I do.

Let's start with a physical description of my office. My room is fairly small and has a couple of overstuffed chairs as well as my own. I've got a desk, a file cabinet, and a white board mounted on one wall. Not many other therapists' offices I've seen have a white board, but I like to illustrate points with drawings or writing. Since I'm a teacher and lecturer as well, it just happens to be my thing. My office is quiet and doesn't have much of a high-tech, business feel. I want it to be modest and not intimidating. I try to create an atmosphere of informality and sanctuary from the world.

My work looks pretty much like a set of extended conversations. It's just me and one other person, or sometimes a couple or family. We sit and talk. I sometimes stand and write on the white board, summarizing what we've said or drawing a diagram to make something clearer. Sometimes clients write on the board or draw pictures on paper with crayons or markers. Sometimes they bring in things they have written, pictures or letters, or even objects of importance to share. They usually do most of the talking. Sometimes I lead relaxation and imagery sessions, or use hypnosis or a more active process. Sometimes we do stretching or movement exercises. We've even been known to talk as we walk around the block or visit places that have been difficult for a client in the past.

What I'm Thinking

When you come into my office, you enter my life and I enter yours. I'm curious about your hopes and dreams, accomplishments and expectations. I know you have come for a reason. In all likelihood, you will call it a "problem." That usually means that something is going on in your life that keeps things from being as you want them to be. You may be having "symptoms" of various sorts, such as fights and arguments with those you love or used to love. Maybe you can't sleep or you are losing interest in the things you used to think mattered. Or maybe someone twisted your arm to come in—maybe it's about making things easier for that person. In any case, "the problem" is keeping you from your dreams.

In an effort to size you up I look for clues to what you're looking for, how you see the problem, what your hopes and fears are, and how best to get you where you want to go. I look for a fit between the skills I have and what you need. I have to ask myself if you'd be better off with me or with someone else.

My Bias

Every therapist has certain biases. Those who were trained in family-system approaches look first for family problems behind the symptoms. They explore early family patterns and current relationships for the causes of your pain. Addiction counselors look first for addictive patterns, denial, and ways your relationships and lifestyle keep you suffering. Analysts explore motives and reasons for the things you do, examining early experiences and unexpressed conflicts for clues. Bias drives therapists' attempts at making sense of the problem. And, do you know what? We tend to find what we're looking for!

Like anyone else, I have my own bias. If you tell me you're depressed, I wonder about what you would like to be doing with your life instead of what you are doing. Sooner or later I'll ask if you're thinking about suicide. If you tell me you are anxious, I'm going to be looking for ways the anxiety is sabotaging your life. My own bias is that our "problems" are sometimes expressions of our deeper selves that are not being heard in any other way. They are often voices from within. I'm also concerned about the way you may be trying unsuccessfully to live out others' expectations of you, so I'll look for cultural, social, or family pressures. While I want your pain to go away, I will be looking for the underlying cause of the pain. I'm looking for why the hurt is there, how it blocks you from living, and what we can do to unlock it.

Much of my professional work focuses on trauma. If you come to me, I will be looking for trauma underlying your problem. If I find it, that fact—and all that I have come to know and understand about trauma—will shape my approach with you.

Issues and Resolution

Uncertainty and change create life problems. Treatment is often focused upon "resolving issues" that follow major changes in a person or the world. Let's look at that phrase more closely, to clarify the language that therapists often use. *Issues* are our ongoing problems of living. Grief, for example, is an issue. If you have lost someone important to you, you have to learn to live without that person. You have to let go of that person enough to be able to open your heart to others. *Unresolved grief* simply means you haven't done that. You remain so attached to the person who was lost that you act as if he or she were still alive or still in your life. If you have *unresolved trauma*, it means you are still suffering so badly that you look, act, and feel as if the trauma were still going on. *Unresolved anger* simply means you are still upset enough over some personal setback or wound that your anger surfaces quickly in other situations. You are unable to put the event aside and live again. Most of us have many low-level issues that preoccupy us and shape our lives. One company I know even sells T-shirts with the logo "I've Got Issues." You and I could both buy one.

Resolution is when you resolve (that is, re-solve, or solve again) the problem. You resolve grief and anger when you let go of your preoccupation with loss and injury. You resolve family fighting when you learn how to avoid slipping into old, unproductive patterns of spiraling hostility. You resolve issues of indecision regarding life direction when you determine what step to take next. This doesn't necessarily mean you fix the world or fix the circumstances in your life that are bringing you pain. However, it does mean you are finally getting to clarity, direction, and peace.

Let's take a look at some specific issues and how therapy can help to resolve them.

Therapy for Fear and Anxiety Caused by Social Uncertainty and Change

Recent events have thrown many people into chronic fear, anxiety, depression, and that elusive sense of dislocation called "angst." Dealing with these reactions has been the focus of much of this book. Sometimes it helps to have another person—particularly one who is trained and skillful—assist you in doing some of the recovery exercises and in dealing with troubling issues. A therapist may be able to help you deal with your particular circumstances more effectively.

Resolving the personal issues created by 9/11, Hurricane Katrina, or the roller-coaster political and economic shifts of the past several years does not mean reinventing history or changing the current global state of affairs. Resolution means learning to handle the feelings of anxiety and fear that can cripple your willingness to continue to invest in your life, and to take the moderate and reasonable risks necessary to grow and thrive. It means learning to live in spite of world events.

Therapy for the Family

The home can be a sanctuary. In the home, family members can find shelter from the storms of the world, acknowledgement of their uniqueness, and support for their process of becoming themselves. The at-home feeling can be a source of comfort and renewal. Or home can be yet another battleground, undermining well-being and individual growth. During times of social stress, the promise of family support can be compromised and destroyed.

Family therapy can be helpful in restoring the nurturing capacity of the home. When family life has degenerated into chronic conflicts, fighting, estrangement, parenting difficulty, rebellion, unwelcome change, specific points of difficulty, or incompatible values or behavior, family therapy may help to restore the balance and calm.

Family therapists help the family rediscover healthy ways of interacting as a family. As a family therapist, I find several themes constantly reoccurring in families that need assistance. My work generally centers upon restoring lines of communication, working out approaches to problem solving, finding ways to resolve conflict and stop unproductive fighting, and creating a climate that honors and appreciates individual difference. Among my client families, work on these issues seems to go the farthest toward restoring family balance. Problem resolution with families means more than stopping the fighting or increasing the communication; it means re-creating the sense of sanctuary that has been lost.

Getting to Peace: Trauma Therapy

If you suffer lasting distress from the overwhelming impact of life's trials and tribulations in the ways outlined in Chapters 5 and 6, you would do well to find a therapist who deals with trauma. Not all therapists are comfortable—or skilled—in dealing with trauma.

Trauma issues—big or little—usually eclipse other issues. Seriously distressing incidents are so life-threatening that our brains prioritize survival over other concerns. Sometimes loss or anger issues are connected to traumatic experiences. In this case, you have to resolve the trauma before you can let go of the anger or loss. Also, resolution of trauma sometimes allows anger and loss issues to surface. It's kind of like peeling onions; you have to get past the hard covering to get to the inside layers. And sometimes you cry.

Trauma therapy is fairly specific in purpose: It is done to relieve the various symptoms we've discussed throughout this book. At its heart, successful trauma treatment involves desensitizing the terrifying and painful feelings associated with traumatic memories. Doing so breaks the cycle of intrusive imagery and resulting arousal reactions. Some approaches have been shown to be very helpful in relieving the suffering and resolving the personal issues surrounding delayed stress reactions. Once therapy succeeds in breaking the imagery-arousal cycle, it can then proceed to secondary issues such as grief, relationship problems, and life changes.

This means that the trauma-therapy process usually isn't simple. It usually involves dealing with uncomfortable stuff; furthermore, things can come up in therapy that we can't always anticipate. Be wary of therapists who claim quick fixes. They often are simply talking about the surface reactions—the outside of the onion. Some new approaches are surprisingly effective at the first level; they even are very useful in dealing strategically with the deeper level. However, if integrating the trauma into your worldview and making meaning of it is on your agenda, expect therapy to take a little longer. In dealing with trauma issues, resolution means placing the events into perspective and into the past. It does not mean forgetting or ignoring; it just means no longer living as if the incident were still happening.

Different Ways to Go

In the sections below I outline some therapeutic approaches that I have found to be useful in therapy for issues stemming from sudden social change, emergency, or trauma situations. A growing body of empirical evidence supports these approaches. It is helpful for you to know their names and a little bit about how they work in order to be able to talk with a therapist. These are not the only therapies that work, simply the ones with whose effectiveness I have firsthand, proven experience.

Cognitive Behavioral Therapy

Cognitive behavioral therapy approaches issues with a focus upon problem solving. This approach is based on the belief that symptoms are undesirable patterns of reacting and behavior. I like to draw a circle on my white board that represents the problematic behavioral pattern. If we can map out the pattern, we can identify ways to interrupt it. I look at the following key points in the cycle of symptomatic behavior:

1. The triggering situation (in the world or in the person's consciousness)

2. The thoughts that shape how the situation is interpreted

3. Specific "self-talk" that furthers the interpretation

4. Feelings that are created in response to the situation, thoughts, and "self-talk"

5. Body reactions to the thoughts and feelings

6. Behaviors that result from the thoughts, feelings, and body reactions

7. The manner in which the behavior makes the overall situation better or worse

Each of these seven stages of the symptomatic behavior is a potential "point of contact" where we may take action in order to break the cycle. We create a plan for becoming more comfortable in the triggering situations, for thinking about the situation differently, and for talking to ourselves differently about it. We find ways to shift feelings and body reactions to the situation. We look at alternative behaviors that break the thought-feeling-body reaction cycle and have a better effect on the triggering situation. (This should all sound familiar from our discussions in Chapters 8, 9, and 10 about ways to deal with acute and delayed reactions to stress.) Cognitive behavioral therapy consists of planning and testing these strategic interventions.

Body Therapy

Sometimes all the thoughts and planning in the world can't touch our re-action patterns. We don't always have conscious access to our deeper-level thoughts and feelings. They simply emerge on their own through bodily, emotional, and behavioral responses in ways that surprise and confuse us. Sometimes thoughts and memories pop up, interrupting our daily life in ways we can't predict or understand. Various therapeutic approaches have been developed to deal directly with these "nonconscious" symptoms.

These bodywork approaches share the belief that the body is key to reaching some of our deepest emotions and memories. Our muscle configurations reflect our emotions. If we are fearful and poised for flight, our bodies carry that tension. Over time these patterns of "holding energy" become fixed and rigid—and so do our underlying body structures. Bodywork works from the muscles themselves inward toward the emotions and memories.

Some time ago a therapist named Ida Rolf developed a technique for releasing feelings through deep tissue massage. The technique is called *Rolfing*. There have been several offshoots of Rolfing over the past few years. One of these was designed by Joseph Heller and is appropriately called *Hellerwork* or *structural integration*. Newer body approaches include *somatic experiencing* and *thought-field therapy*. Like bodywork, these techniques involve direct intervention with body-energy patterns in order to release symptoms that resist change. Research supporting the use of these approaches is promising.

One of the frustrations I experienced working with trauma cases was roadblocks. Sometimes, using cognitive or even expressive approaches, the client and I reached a point where we had gained insight and awareness but couldn't achieve change. The client's progress would plateau, and we would be stymied by intense emotional responses to images. These would not go away through either perspective or understanding. I began incorporating into my practice a form of therapy known as *eye-movement desensitization and reprocessing (EMDR)*, which I found useful in breaking through these "stuck" periods. It seemed to somehow desensitize painful memories and help restore the client's sense of self-control and feelings of well-being, helping him or her to move beyond the limitations set by entrenched fear and avoidance.

Expressive or Narrative Therapy

Art and dance therapies have established impressive track records for helping people get in touch with memories and feelings related to trauma. More importantly, they go beyond symptom management. The expressive therapies help explore the meaning of the incident and integrate the experience into ongoing life. They don't wait for talk, although talk often follows the movement or art making. In dance and movement therapy, physical movement explores and releases feeling and awareness. In art therapy, the work itself records the experience and becomes the object of discussion.

The "new" expressive therapy is writing. In a surprising set of studies, writing was shown to be as effective as talk therapy in terms of symptom reduction and general health. As in any new approach, specific guidelines for the therapeutic use of writing are under construction. I have found writing very helpful with my clients, particularly when it taps into the power of classic narrative structure and mythic form. Other ways I have used it clinically have included guided journal, letter, and song writing. I find the *Creative Journal* workbooks of Dr. Lucia Capacchione particularly helpful for many of my clients. The "Things to Think and Write About" sections in this book offer writing exercises that are designed to help you relate your experiences and make sense of them.

My approach to doing therapy is eclectic. I blend cognitive behavioral therapy, body therapy, and expressive/narrative therapy. I also use EMDR strategically, to break through blocks. Each approach works differently, and each client differs in need. My strategies depend upon the clients' needs and style, the stage of therapy they are in, and the particular task they face. Again, these are definitely not the only therapies that are effective; they are simply the approaches I find most useful in my setting.

Shop Around

Become familiar with different approaches to therapy. Consumer magazines often contain articles about therapies. The psychology and self-help sections of bookstores are overflowing with resources. Network; talk to friends who have been in therapy about therapists they found helpful. Develop a list of questions to ask a therapist when you first meet him or her. Such a list might include the following:

- Do you have experience treating clients who have undergone trauma?

- What approaches do you use?

- Are you comfortable dealing with _____?

- Do you incorporate writing or artwork in your treatment?

- How long do you anticipate the therapy process taking?

- What do you see to be reasonable goals for our efforts?

- How will we know when we meet those goals, or when the therapy process isn't working?

- How much do you charge?

A Few Words about Medication

Don't expect a therapist to do what a medical doctor does. If you have a headache, doctors can give you a pill that will fix the headache. They can give you pills to put you to sleep, make you numb, or lift your spirits, but they can't give you a pill to fix what's making your heart ache. Medicine can put off suffering for a while, but there is no antibiotic that can cure an imbalance of the soul.

That doesn't mean there is no place for medication in the treatment of reactions to significant distress. Some chemical imbalances that result in symptoms can be made more manageable with medication. The proper use of medication is not to fix the problem—that's a given—but to lower the intensity of symptom spirals enough so that therapy has a chance to work. Another way medication can be used is in cases of "dual diagnosis." If you are suffering from another mental disorder that can be addressed by medication, doing so may allow treatment to progress. Talk to both your doctor and your therapist to work out a sensible approach.

Choosing for Fit

Beyond the therapist's bias and style regarding his or her approach, what matters most is who the therapist is. Not only are you going to spend some time with this person, you're going to spill some pretty important beans. Can this person be trusted with your feelings? Do you feel more comfortable with a man or woman? Does this person appear trustworthy? Going beyond your initial worry, does this person look like someone in whom you can confide? If not, don't go there. If after a couple of sessions you have reservations about opening your heart to this person, move on. But be aware that you have to balance in your mind two impulses in making this decision. If you feel reluctance, is your reluctance based upon distrust of this particular person or upon a deeper unwillingness to deal with the issues? It is frightening to open up to anyone. Does this person look like an ally in the process or an obstacle?

As a final word, allow me to repeat an important point: There are different kinds of therapy, and different reasons for doing therapy. Relational problems, behavior and habit control, anxiety and depression management, existential concerns, and personal-growth issues are all good reasons to go into therapy, but these various issues may dictate what kind of therapy—and what kind of therapist—to try.

THINGS TO THINK AND WRITE ABOUT

- Have you gotten to the point of realizing that your problem is bigger than you are?

- Is your reluctance to see a professional simply a matter of false pride?

- Have you considered looking at the problem like a business expense: What is holding onto and ignoring the problem costing you in terms of lost life?

- What is your problem costing those around you?

- If you were to seek out a professional, who might you network with in order to locate an appropriate one?

CHAPTER 13

Reconnecting
with
Loved Ones

"Welcome home, brother." This simple phrase in certain contexts has a special meaning. Among Vietnam veterans it has come to suggest the end of an exile. Many vets suffered recurrent bouts of posttraumatic stress and alienation left over from their wartime experiences. They left for a controversial war and returned to a divided nation and a divided self. Many bore injuries, and some of those were hidden. The sorts of social support they had expected to be available for their recovery did not exist. In their heads and hearts they remained somewhere else, haunted by what they had been a part of, what they had done, and what they had become. Consequently, those Vietnam veterans suffered high rates of divorce. Preliminary studies show a similar social disconnect between soldiers returning from Middle East combat and the society that sent them.

Anyone who has been through a life-changing event—a major loss, a social upheaval, or victimization—has experienced a similar exile. Whether or not things in the home or the world have changed, the person has changed inside. If you have been through an experience serious enough to have left you with anger, fear, sadness, depression, or dissociation, you may have as much difficulty returning "home" as a soldier returning from the battlefield. The current social confusion and uncertainty has brought this sense of dislocation home to us all. Many of us struggle to return to the relationships we had before things became unsettled.

The Greek poet Homer, writing at the time when oral tradition was being encoded into written language, captures a theme that has passed down through countless retellings and still remains profound. He tells the story of Ulysses (sometimes called Odysseus), king of Ithaca, and of his arduous journey home from the Trojan War. Ulysses goes through more turmoil trying to get home than he encountered in battle. He arrives back in Ithaca ten years after the war's end, wearing a disguise, and finds the place in disarray. He has been assumed dead, and his wife is besieged by suitors competing for his place in her bed and on his throne. Even though Ulysses has entered the gates, he still has to win back Penelope.

The story of Ulysses is not just a story about war. It is an account of someone who has to fight to return to a place from which he was taken by unforeseen events that changed him. On a psychological level, it is the story of everyone who has been changed by events and who seeks to return to a real or psychological "home." Literature is full of characters standing outside the door of their homes, unable to enter.

On the Outside Looking In

Tragedies, traumas, and periods of social upheaval throw us out of our homes. I'm not talking about the buildings we occupy. We are left standing outside of ourselves. Our world shifts, and so do our expectations and feelings of place. We lose our sense of knowing where our sanctuary lies. As we struggle to regain our lives after major upsets, we are like Ulysses returning home, unsure how to reclaim the relationships that sustain us.

Soldiers returning from battle bring the war home with them, like the mud on their boots. They bring images and memories, but also new sets of reflexes and expectations. They bring a sense of horror and sadness at what they have seen and what they have learned. These changes separate them from those they love. Similarly, in the aftermath of social difficulty and rapid change, like returning soldiers, we cannot tell what we have seen because words cannot go there. We carry a frightening knowledge in our hearts that we cannot convey. We are filled with images, memories, reflexes, and expectations that keep us apart from our loved ones and them apart from us. We become strangers in our own homes.

Coming home means recapturing the at-home feeling that is missing. It means resetting our internal balance and renegotiating our external relationships. Coming home requires new ways of relating and of living. Although we may never get back to the place we left, our task is to construct a new way of being there.

My, How You've Changed

When we undergo serious, life-changing events, we don't feel like ourselves. More importantly, we don't act like ourselves. All of the stress and trauma symptoms we have talked about in the preceding chapters amount to changes in our behavior. We don't walk, talk, think, or relate to others as we did before. From the perspective of those around us, we have disappeared, and only a reminder of our former self remains. Like Ulysses, the person who shows up is in disguise. Our friends and loved ones try to adjust to this changed person but, like Penelope, they are stuck living with a stranger and waiting for the return of the person they loved.

Certain feelings and behaviors are normal in the aftermath of crisis. They are the result of healthy people being affected by unhealthy situations. They can sometimes include

- helplessness
- explosiveness
- impatience
- defensiveness
- dishonesty

- impulsiveness
- distrust
- destructiveness
- irresponsibility
- fear

- jealousy
- rage
- perfectionism
- false pride
- false humility

No matter how normal and expected these feelings and behaviors may be, they are hard for others to live with. Even harder to live with are destructive attitudes that can become entrenched over time. The longer it takes to recover from a crisis, the more ingrained these attitudes become. Such attitudes may include

- resentment
- contempt
- paranoia
- arrogance
- pessimism

- intolerance
- criticalness
- skepticism
- envy
- judgment

- distrust
- self-centeredness
- unforgivingness
- aloofness
- punitiveness

Even the best relationships become stressed when toxic feelings, behaviors and attitudes undermine trust and create mutual defensiveness.

It's uncomfortable to hold these attitudes and have them guide our actions, but it's even worse to try to live with someone who holds them. When we are consumed with these attitudes, we hurt those closest to us the most.

Our silences, our agitation and fading away, our hypervigilance and preoccupation all conspire to erode the trust necessary to sustain close relationships. Adjustment and reconstruction of trust take time. The optimism and joy we shared and the comfort we found within our relationships can turn to frustration and sadness under the weight of pro longed, drawn-out healing. Penelope becomes bitter and tires of waiting, while Ulysses haunts the palace grounds, unrecognizable in his disguise.

Helping Loved Ones

There are steps you can take during your return home to ease tensions and buffer those you love. The most important one is to let them know what has happened to you. If they are aware of the effect of the event upon you, that you are suffering, that your behavior is caused by your suffering rather than by something they did or by how you feel about them, and if they know that you are trying to make things better, it can help greatly. Give them a reason to endure the hardship, and they will be better able to wait for you. It's not a fix, but it will buy time.

People who love you need to know where you have been and where you are right now. Of course you haven't figured all that out, but they need to have progress reports along the way. The following are some suggestions for keeping your loved ones in the loop:

— Keep your expectations in check. Don't assume that just because you are trying, they are getting all they need. Telling them as much as you can is simply a start for them, just as it is for you.

— Describe to them your basic experiences. Keep it fairly simple. Don't overwhelm them with all the gory details. Remember that what you experienced can also be upsetting to them. Outline the facts of the incident(s), but describe the upsetting parts indirectly. If your incident involved physical mutilation, for instance, just say that. Instead of, "I saw blood, entrails, decapitation, etc.," keep it to, "I saw people hurt very badly."

— Focus instead upon what the event *meant* to you. Describe your feelings and reactions.

— Tell them about your continuing reactions. Use feeling words as much as you can. If you are experiencing nightmares and flash-backs, use general terms. Say, "I keep seeing it happen again," rather than describing the specific visual content. Again, let them know the effect the flashbacks have on you. Use language like: "And when I see it again, I get so upset I can't say any-thing."

— Spend time describing how your reactions interfere with your relationship with them. Let them know how your times of with-drawal or upset are about your trying to control yourself, not about how you feel about them.

— Tell them what you are doing to get better, and let them know how they can help. Ask them to be patient during your recovery process.

— Ask them how your behavior affects them. See if there are ways you could handle your continued distress that would be easier on them.

More ways exist to reassure your loved ones and thus buy some time for your recovery. Use the strategies for staying centered that we discussed in Chapters 8, 9, and 10. If in the middle of encounters with your partner or family members you find yourself becoming agitated or fading out, take the appropriate countermeasures to remain in the present. Try to figure out if some of the issues causing difficulties in your relationship might be related to the crisis. Work with a therapist—either alone or as a family or couple—if it feels right to do so.

Another thing you can do to maintain your relationships during the process of healing is to take care of yourself. The following are some sug-gestions for doing so:

— Make sure you are following an appropriate stress-manage-ment program. Reasonable rest, diet, and exercise are minimum daily requirements for supporting personal recovery and interpersonal growth.

— It often helps to talk to people who know you and the relation-ship you are in. They may be able to help you gain perspective on what is and isn't important or what is reasonable to expect of yourself and your partner. Consider talking to trusted friends, clergy, or a counselor.

— Try to sit down and clarify your responsibilities with the friends, family members, or business partners to whom you feel you owe something. Find out exactly what they expect from you. Your feelings of responsibility may be exaggerated. It may be that they see things differently. Be open to possibilities for negotiating.

— Get clear within yourself how you would like things to be and what sorts of compromises you are willing to make in handling your relationships with others. It helps to know what you want before you try to work out agreements and understandings with others at home, on the job, or in the community.

— If you feel that you have overwhelming responsibilities, you are probably right. Look at how you prioritize your work and family time. Are all of your responsibilities of equal importance to you? Is there some way you could better organize your time commitments and deploy your energy to reflect your priorities? Try listing your major priorities on paper. Reorder them in terms of their importance to you. In another column, list the major complications and stressors that keep you from accomplishing them. Are there actions you could take to minimize some of the complications? Look for ways to put less time and energy into meeting the less important responsibilities and commitments, and ways to put more time and energy into meeting the more important ones.

— Consider taking daily time for yourself, doing things you like, or even taking a short vacation by yourself. There is an old saying: "The more we do what we've always done, the more we get what we always got." Sometimes we become so caught up in family struggles that we exhaust ourselves and continually make things worse. If you are having difficulty detaching from family drama, perhaps you could take a little time off and spend it enriching your life and recharging your batteries. You may be more effective in connecting with your family if you allow yourself some time alone.

— If you are having problems reconnecting, try approaching family activities differently. Prepare yourself before you try to reconnect with family members. Think through what you want to happen, what has gone wrong before, and how you wish to approach it differently this time. If you find things becoming too intense during your attempts at reconnection, excuse yourself for short breathers, and practice the steps listed in Chapter 8 to manage the stress. Finally, talk over the experience afterward with someone you trust to make sense of how it went.

When They Are Part of the Problem

As you deal with problem feelings and behaviors that result from major upset, your partner may lose patience. It's hard to live with someone who seems chronically angry, fearful, depressed, or disconnected. If your partner runs out of coping energy, you may find yourself dealing with relational problems, on top of problems arising from your crisis experience. The following are some suggestions for dealing with problem partners:

Look beyond your partner's behavior and see the need. When people are being difficult, it is usually because they feel they are bearing an unfair burden within the relationship. If you are suffering from postcrisis aftershocks, your partner probably *is* bearing an unfair burden: *you*. Rather than getting hung up in guilt, focus upon figuring out what he or she needs. It may be security, attention, or something else.

Reassure your partner, based on the real need. What could you say or do that would address your partner's need directly without compromising your own needs? Often, well-chosen time together can provide reassurance that the other person remains important to you.

Hang tough. Recovery takes time, and relational recovery takes even more time. Changes in feelings and behavior—even changes for the better—constitute changes in the relationship. This involves breaches of an unspoken contract between you, issues of trust, and shifting expectations. It takes a while to get used to a "new normal." Don't assume these changes will come quickly and flawlessly.

Mobilize support for yourself outside the relationship. You need other people to listen, share your struggles, and suggest alternatives. Don't expect your relationship to meet all these needs when the relationship itself is under pressure. Seek support from extended family, friends, and professionals.

Healing Your Relationships by Making Amends

Consider the position of someone close to you. Your relationship may have been strained by actions that were caused by the ordeal you are struggling to overcome. Your loved ones may have been visited by blow-back they didn't deserve. While this is not your fault, it is your responsibility. If you want to retake control of your relationships and your fate, you must rebuild the bridges that connect you and those you love. Consider using the following process of making amends to repair and renew relationships.

First, start with self-assessment. Take seriously what others are saying. Set aside your rationalizations, and look at your behavior. How have your actions since the incident affected others? Ask yourself the following questions, and consider writing your answers in a journal:

- Have your reactions to circumstances changed?
- Are you being inconsistent in your actions and reactions?
- Have you failed to follow through on promises?
- Have you failed to be the support for loved ones that you need them to be for you?
- Have you been moody, irritable, reclusive, or extra needy?
- Have you been trying to cover up your feelings and actions?
- Are you violating your own past standards and values?
- Is your behavior volatile and unpredictable?
- Have you fallen into a pattern of blaming those around you for your distress?
- Are you less open to the needs of those around you?

If your answer to some of these is yes, this is perfectly understandable, perhaps even inevitable, following a serious life upset. Still, changes in your behavior are hard on others. Not only that, they have the unintended effect of driving others away and compounding your isolation. You need your significant relationships to help you heal.

Whenever we bring pain to others, we put ourselves off balance. Our actions cut two ways: In hurting others, we lose our own sense of integrity. We experience guilt and shame. If you are to regain peace of mind and heal your relationships, you must right the wrongs you have committed. The specific wrongs are unique to your situation, but many people who are recovering from difficult life events report patterns of

- intolerance
- breaking promises
- helplessness
- jealousy
- abuse
- immorality
- being highly controlling

- irresponsibility
- fighting
- explosiveness
- dishonesty
- chronic arguing
- name-calling
- making incessant demands

- displaced anger
- overworking
- withdrawal
- self-centeredness
- substance abuse
- being insulting
- being an embarrassment

Making amends is one of the most powerful tools you have to turn the situation around. Through the amends-making process, you defuse the shame that constricts you, set the stage for reconstructing healthy relationships, and open yourself to a future full of new possibilities.

Making amends consists of acknowledgment, apology, and restitution. The first step involves a frank admission that you did these things and that the responsibility for doing them is yours. This lets the other person know that you are not blaming him or her.

Apology is the formal expression of regret, remorse, and a request for forgiveness. It's important to remember, however, that whether the other person grants forgiveness is entirely up to him or her. You can't control another's response to your making amends, and your inner work may entail letting go of needing him or her to forgive you. Just because you make formal amends doesn't mean another "owes" you forgiveness or even appreciation for your efforts. The important thing from your point of view is that you have honestly and fully owned up to your part in the problems between you. Whatever the other person's response to your making amends, acknowledgement and apology help restore personal dignity to him or her, as well as to you. They set the stage for rebuilding the relationship by acknowledging obligation and intent to change.

Restitution involves repairing the damage. If something is broken, it must be fixed. Losses must be paid back when possible. Some damages are irreparable, but time or effort spent may be acceptable restitution. Spending a day or a week working on a project, or devoting time and attention to someone you've neglected, may show that person what your words cannot tell. Because each situation differs, you may need to be creative in finding ways to make restitution. Symbolic restitution is important to both of you, even if full payback is impossible.

Sometimes making amends can cause further harm. Normally, making amends includes full disclosure of the damaging act. But if full disclosure would cause further unnecessary hurt, it should not be made. In such cases, partial disclosure—leaving out the damaging material—may be appropriate.

In any case, making amends is only part of the process. Saying you're sorry isn't enough, even with full restitution. Restitution can best be made by inflicting no further damage—that is, by displaying more loving, considerate, moderate, and responsible behavior henceforth.

Ulysses and the Road Home

Literary scholars and psychologists find much of interest in the story of Ulysses. To get home from the war, Ulysses sailed through many challenges. He was cursed by the gods after the war and endured suffering and being blown far off course. Probably the most telling part of his odyssey for our purposes is its ending.

When Ulysses finally reached Ithaca, he found it under siege. As the story goes, his wife Penelope had given up hope that Ulysses would return and agreed to marry the suitor who could bend Ulysses' bow and fire an arrow through a set of axe rings—a feat that only Ulysses had performed. Ulysses, in disguise, took his place among the suitors. When his chance came, he bent the bow, put the arrow through the axe rings, and proceeded to clean out the palace with the help of his son and some friends. Thus, he reclaimed his wife and throne.

Until he picked up his bow, Ulysses was unable to reclaim his life. What significance does the bow have in this story, and in your story and mine?

The bow was made just for Ulysses, to fit his reach, his strength, and his knowledge. It was a tool only he could use. Others could only approximate his skill with it and they failed. The bow represented Ulysses' true path and his true self. For Ulysses to pick up his bow was for him to be what only he could be.

For you to come home, you must rediscover who you are. You must recapture your sense of identity and direction. Your desires, strengths, values, and goals are yours alone. They may be disguised by the aftershocks of the overwhelming event—by your newly found fears, confusions, and preoccupations—but they form the substrate of your identity. We do not live in a vacuum; rather, we live in relationship to others. Coming home means bringing your true self home and taking your place among those you love. Coming home means taking up your bow again, and rediscovering and redefining your original path.

THINGS TO THINK AND WRITE ABOUT

- Is there someone in your life who has reacted to your behavior by going "absent without leave"?

- Is your life richer or poorer without that person?

- What issues—things that divided you—still remain painful?

- Are you willing to set those issues aside or to find new balance within yourself so that those issues can be laid to rest?

- What concrete steps can you take to rebuild bridges?

CHAPTER 14

Rebuilding the Spirit

Many of us feel that our world is spinning off course. Terror, economic and political instability, globalization, environmental decline, media hysteria, and a host of other disquieting forces conspire to push us off balance at the personal level. We struggle with the toxic beliefs and attitudes generated by widespread fear and chronic, low-level trauma. We do not want to slide into distrust, hostility, and cynicism, but it is hard to remain cheerful, trusting, and generous if we do not feel safe. While the world spins uncertainly, we grapple with the spiritual challenges of meaninglessness, isolation, fragmentation, and futility.

We need to take action to reinforce and rebuild our spirit if we are to avoid despair. Renewal doesn't just happen, particularly in the face of continuous erosion. In order to build our spiritual resilience, we must make an intentional and sustained effort. The best way to do so is also the most obvious. For thousands of years people have engaged in deliberate spiritual practice.

Developing a Personal Spiritual Practice

Whatever your religious beliefs—or lack thereof—you will probably benefit from an active practice to counter the effects of spiritual depletion. A spiritual practice activates the higher awareness and internal resources you need to ward off fear and alienation. You can blend into one of the many forms of practice or worship that churches or more secular institutions in your community provide, you can turn to customs you have found helpful in the past, or you can develop new ways that better fit your needs today.

The purpose of spiritual practice is to regain internal balance and to put yourself into a healthy relationship with the external world. Whether you walk your own path or join with others, there are several elements of spiritual practice that have proved helpful to many throughout human history. As you seek the right practice for yourself, consider the following general approaches.

Find Sanctuary

Everybody needs a place where there is relief from the countless pressures of telephones, noise, and others who demand attention. Although places of worship often provide such a haven, many people find refuge in their study, in an art studio, or outside in a natural setting. Your sanctuary should be a place that allows you contemplation and reflection, undisturbed by the normal demands of life.

Pray, Meditate, or Engage in Meaningful Ritual

The soul requires peace. For some, this means a vocal dialogue with their God. For others, it means clearing their minds and opening themselves to deeper levels of awareness. For still others, it requires an opportunity for creative expression or to reconnect with their bodies through rest or physical activity. For many, it means a specific, predictable ritual. A great many practice with others of like disposition, while some prefer to practice alone. The main thing is to provide yourself with a means of connecting with yourself in ways that your daily routine does not allow.

Open Your Heart and Reflect

The world is full of distractions; it pulls you away from yourself and toward others' agendas for you. A good spiritual practice helps you reawaken to your own inner experience and allows you to reevaluate your relationship to the world. It helps you find a balance between the demands of life and your own deeper needs.

Does your spiritual practice help you meet your higher needs? Does it help you sort out the nature of your life, its purpose, and the quality of your connection with others? Does it help you decide what you need to do to be true to yourself, and does it empower you to walk that path?

Look to Feelings and Experience Rather than Concepts and Beliefs

Find a practice that *feels* right for you, rather than one that *sounds* right to others. Many people define spirituality as a set of right beliefs. They spend a great deal of energy trying to convince you that their way of seeing things is the right way. Remember to look beyond the concepts and beliefs to the core experience of the practice. Does it help you to find your center? Does something deep inside of you respond, and do you feel more like yourself in a real way as a result of engaging with it?

The Goals of Spiritual Renewal

Whatever form of spiritual practice you engage in, use it to work at overcoming the four great threats to personal fulfillment: isolation, meaninglessness, powerlessness, and personal fragmentation. The rest of this chapter suggests ways to meet these core goals within a spiritual practice. Consider writing about your thoughts as you reflect on the material presented.

Reconnect

As you are pulled into the ongoing drama of the world, you can lose touch with yourself and with those who are most important to you. You risk a pervading sense of personal isolation. You can lose your sense of the world, of your relationship to the earth, and of your tie to a power greater than yourself. Reconnection to all of these is central to your well-being.

Rediscover Your Body

Your physical body is your link to the world; it grounds you in the present when your mind is stuck in ruminating about the past or imagining the future. By shifting consciousness to your body, you can become at one with yourself; use sensory enjoyment, relaxation, movement, dance, or even simple walking. Many people find they can use active meditation—such as tai chi or a walking meditation—to enhance their awareness of themselves and the world in the here and now.

Connect with Your Deeper Self

You are more than your surface thoughts, feelings, and desires. Like most people, during your early development you learned to hide the parts of yourself you felt others would reject. Those estranged parts now clamor to be heard. They can be a source of unanticipated strength and richness. Many people have learned to be sensitive to their unguarded thoughts and feelings. Through their waking images and nighttime dreams, artwork and writing, observation of their unconscious behavior, and feedback from trusted others, they discover things about themselves they didn't know. By opening to your deeper self, you open new possibilities of living.

Strengthen Family and Friendships

Times of uncertainty and stress can cause you to withdraw from others, even those from whom you receive support and comfort. You may do this unconsciously because you feel you can't bear to care anymore. Perhaps you fear risking the loss of those you love, and think, "Why invest in something that may only bring pain?" But if you withdraw from others, you cut yourself off from a vital lifeline. It is only through acknowledging the importance of others and working at reconnection that you can gain the support you—and they—need.

Reconnect with Those from Whom You Have Become Estranged

When people are afraid and angry they tend to strike out at those closest to them. Thus, your family and closest friends can end up being the unwilling recipients of bad feelings engendered within you by the world. This can drive wedges into the best of relationships. If you have pulled away from someone you treasure, now is the time to rebuild that important connection. Look past your internal ledger of accumulated slights and injustices. Focus upon the other person's importance and needs rather than on your own hurt. Practice forgiveness as a form of self-healing rather than as charity. Your forgiving past transgressions does not mean you feel the other person's actions were right; it just means you choose to let go of the pain.

Connect with the Higher Power Within

Whether you believe in a white-bearded God who rules the universe, a whole set of gods, or no God at all, understand that there is within you a power and perspective that can transcend the daily confusion and discomforts of this world. It really doesn't matter whether this higher power inside you is the hand of God within, a cultural archetype hardwired into your brain, or simply a different and broader state of mind. The fact is that this divine spark is a resource close at hand. Learn to recognize it, listen to it, and nurture it. If you are troubled by the state of the world, beset by fears and anger, and haunted by ghosts from the past, this higher power within is a stabilizing force available for you now.

Engage in Your Practice Regularly

If you do something regularly, it becomes part of your life. This is as true for developing your spiritual capacity as it is for playing the piano or swinging a golf club. Practice may not make perfect, but it does make for integration. When you practice a new skill regularly, it becomes you. You have a spiritual self—a set of strengths and resources within that can help you through times of need—and connecting with this spiritual self takes practice. Through customary rituals, meditation, or prayers, you evoke and exercise your spiritual power and it becomes a guiding factor in your daily life.

Connect with a Spiritual Community

It is easier to become attuned to spirituality when others acknowledge, support, and provide a context for your process. Religious groups are built for this, although they differ greatly in approach and style. If you are a member of one, consider rethinking how you participate, and explore ways in which you might revitalize your involvement. If you are thinking about joining a religious organization, do some serious shopping around. One size does not fit all; find one that feels right for you. Finally, you may be the sort of person who can't relate to organized religion. Churches have no exclusive corner on the spirituality market, so look for other groups—formal or informal—that will provide support for your spiritual search.

Sharpen Your Sense of Purpose

A wise friend who was getting a bit eccentric in his older years would stop people on the street and announce to them, "You are walking toward your destiny!" However odd and inappropriate he appeared to other, more conventional folks, he was right. Our actions manifest our purpose. It isn't so much where we *intend* to go with our lives but where we end up walking that counts. Our plans and intentions, however, can provide direction.

The military has missiles that are guided by heat sensors. They automatically follow the high temperatures generated by the target's exhaust. In similar fashion, we humans are meaning-seeking missiles. You and I seek significance. We look for the underlying order in the world and seek out projects and goals that make sense of our lives. We follow trails of meaning that make our lives purposeful. A famous psychotherapist who survived the death camps of World War II once observed that people who have a strong enough reason *to* live could survive almost any circumstances *of* living. When we lose our direction, when we begin to experience our lives as having no purpose and the universe as having no order, we risk collapse into meaninglessness. In the face of a capricious world we must double our efforts to rediscover the path of our heart.

Refine Your Sense of Direction

Where are you headed? Often it isn't so much that we have lost or run out of direction as it is that we have forgotten it. When we're young, our idea of direction is more general. As we mature, sometimes it gets lost in the various twists and turns we have taken in its pursuit. We wander the world mistaking the means toward the goal for the goal itself.

Review Your Vocational Path

Think about where you have been going. Has your path taken you where you intended? Life lays down surprises. An expected opening does not materialize. An unanticipated opportunity opens up. Our lives seem to be an interplay between intent and fortune, sometimes creating paths that meander in ways we could never predict. Is the work you do in keeping with your original intent? A related question: Have you fallen short of your original intent, met it, or surpassed it? The underlying issue for all of us is whether we have unfinished personal agendas regarding our work in the world.

Reconcile Work with Purpose

No matter how you got to your current work situation, does it provide you with a sense of direction and meaning? If your job is intrinsically worthwhile, if it allows you a sense that what you are doing is important, rejoice! If it falls short of that, however, understand that it is costing you on a spiritual level to keep doing it. Consider the wisdom of keeping your current job; maybe it is time to move on. Sometimes the bottom line, however, is that you simply can't quit doing what you are doing because it feeds your family and pays the rent or mortgage. In this case, the work does have meaning because it serves another purpose. Through it, you are able to keep your promises to those you love. Further, your job may also serve as a staging area for more important work outside the job.

Develop Purposeful Pursuits Outside of Your Job

Your job is not necessarily your real work. For some people, a job is simply a way to make money. Your real work in the world—that which brings you a true sense of accomplishment and satisfaction—may be entirely different. Still, your employment may do more than simply feed you and your family; it may also provide you with the resources and means to do the thing to which you feel called. Many artists, for example, work at a normal job in order to free their art from the pressures of the marketplace and allow it to find its highest expression. The bottom line is this: If you find that you are underemployed, or that your job does not provide you with a sense of joy and fulfillment, the answer may be to develop a meaningful pursuit outside your job. Making this pursuit possible may be a major purpose of your job.

Strengthen Your Awareness of Meaning in the World

It isn't always your work or relationships that feel meaningless. Sometimes it is the world itself. Particularly when things are changing rapidly, it is tempting to see the world as chaotic and without meaning. It is important to remember that this attitude is as much about your own way of seeing as it is about the world. We all see according to habit. We see in part what we expect to see. Like the turning of tides, the changing of seasons, and falling in and out of love, some of the most powerful forces in the world are the most subtle. Deeper awareness of the world requires new levels of perception. Through practice and attunement, you can learn to see with your heart and your bones, not just your mind.

Regain a Sense of Personal Effectiveness

In a culture that sees us primarily as consumers, it is easy to feel a loss of personal importance. Powerful forces of influence are brought to bear to convince us that by purchasing this product, watching that movie, or voting for this candidate, we are actually having some effect in the world. This passive, false, marketplace-driven consciousness robs us of true participation in shaping our own world. Part of personal renewal involves regaining real effectiveness.

We often find ourselves falling wide of our mark because we headed off in the wrong direction. As helmsmen on ships discover, a variance of only a few degrees over time can take a ship miles off course. On the other hand, it is even more important to chase the right target in the first place. In assessing whether or not you are carrying out your purpose—being effective—you have to be clear about which benchmarks are true indicators of success. It is wise to periodically check out whether the objectives you have set and the criteria you use to judge completion are really true indicators of progress toward meeting your goals. This is particularly the case with goals you may have adopted when you were relatively young. Sometimes the most important thing you can do to measure your effectiveness is to reexamine whether your goals were wisely chosen.

Explore Inner Resources

We all have within ourselves a host of strengths and skills that we can draw upon when needed. Some are obvious, such as "people skills," intelligence, or drive. Others are less obvious, like resilience, tenacity, forbearance, patience, resolve, understanding, compassion, and honesty. These resources are sometimes "forgotten" during times when they are not needed. They may be needed now. Find a way to review the dormant resources within you. Write about the positive times in your past. Talk to people who knew you "back when." Reexamine the personal strengths you exercised in the past that could be called upon again now.

Accept Your Limits

The first line of a St. Francis prayer made famous by Alcoholics Anonymous asks for the serenity to "accept the things I cannot change." These powerful words point to the fact that there are limits to our abilities. We are children of a flawed world; we simply cannot do all we could, should, and would do if we were perfect. The point is self-acceptance, not aspirations. We must judge ourselves by who we are and what we do rather than by our fantasies of what might be. By the same token, however, our reach is guided by imagination. We can let our aspirations and actions be informed and guided by our dreams. Rather than becoming mired in self-doubt and condemnation, accept your own flaws and those of the world as a realistic and strategic starting point. As beginning writers are frequently advised to do, start where you are.

Balance Work and Play

Play is the heart singing. It is critical to your creativity and effectiveness that you spend some time just "doing nothing." All work and all serious-ness do make us dull. But while play is a good and essential thing, the best play is that which is authentic. Remember that a great many people make a great deal of money pandering to your need for play. Keep your playing in balance, or it can become addictive. Balance your play with reflection on how you spend your time. Are you spending a reasonable amount of time in pursuit of the things of real value?

Out of the Monastery and into the Street

As Thomas Paine said, "These are the times that try men's (and women's) souls." In this sense, the current worldwide instability and uncertainty provide us an unparalleled opportunity for personal growth. When else might we find the impetus to shake loose from our complacence and refine our spiritual capacities?

A spiritual practice provides discipline and focus. It does not have to be the discipline and focus of a monastery, however. Consider a seed. You have only to plant the seed in fertile soil, give it enough water, and keep the temperature neither too hot nor too cold, and the seed will germinate and grow on its own. A spiritual practice does not have to be elaborate or difficult. The goal of having a spiritual practice is simply to provide the conditions necessary to cultivate a sense of connection, purpose, integrity, and effectiveness. After all, what could be more important than a real and meaningful connection with others, our deeper self, and our higher power? What could we possibly wish for our children more than a sense of guiding purpose, personal integrity, and the power to carry out their destiny? Spirituality can infuse your life and strengthen you if you allow it to thrive.

Living with the Truth

When Los Angeles art critic Christopher Knight reviewed British painter Lucien Freud's retrospective exhibit, he observed that Freud's figurative paintings all seemed to expose the limitations of the people he portrayed. Knight wrote, "Ecco Homo—*Behold the Man*—[Freud's] pictures say again and again."

"Behold the man." The New Testament attributes this derisive comment to the ruler Pontius Pilate, who was mocking Christ's suffering and mortality. Pilate is saying, "You are simply a man, not a god."

As humans we are not perfect, and our world is not perfect. Unlike our images of the divine, we are not all-seeing, all-knowing, all-good. Our vision and judgment are limited, as is our capacity to fix things that go wrong. Our grandest projects have underlying flaws. Our bodies fail us, and we occasionally fail each other.

Tragedy

Shakespeare loved a good tragedy. His dark stories have passed the test of time. Why do they remain popular? Because Shakespeare—like the artist Lucien Freud—touches the eternal within us. Tragedy, he shows again and again, is one of the central truths of the human condition.

Bad things happen. People go broke, lose loves, crash dreams, and finally die. But that's not the point of tragedy. The great message of tragedy is the poignancy of it all. Tragedy is more than simple bad news. Tragedy is bad news that is partly of our own making. Specifically, it is when our internal flaws bring about our own unhappiness. *Hamlet*, one of Shakespeare's finest tragedies, culminates in more than simply the deaths of all of the main players—the important people in Hamlet's life. The tragedy of *Hamlet* is that in spite of his noble intentions, most of those deaths result from Hamlet's personal conflicts and mishandling of circumstances.

We are coming to understand that the new age of anxiety we face has tragic dimensions. No matter how clearly we can name perpetrators and place blame, our current predicament is partly a state of our own creation. We got here ourselves, fueled by an unsteady mix of fear, pride, and short-sighted interference on all sides. A long history of good, as well as bad, intentions have mixed like baking soda and vinegar to produce a volcanic eruption. Events in the world seem to be lurching out of balance and control. The world is convulsing, and we feel as if we are along for a very rough ride. Now, in the face of such tragedy, what do we do?

Old answers don't seem to be working. Ignoring the international and domestic situations and carrying on as if nothing were happening seems to be less the answer, and more the problem. Stock political and lifestyle answers that have worked in the past seem both inadequate and inflammatory. The angst setting in upon us brings us face-to-face with fundamental questions regarding our place in the world and our manner of living in it. We need more than the external things the world can provide.

The Fundamental War Within

Some call the events unfolding in the world today a religious war. Some call it a war between capital-based global imperialism and local self-determination. Others feel it is a class struggle between "haves" and "have-nots," even within our own borders. Be that as it may, it is becoming increasingly clear that there is a more profound war at hand.

Outer struggles mask a profound internal division. The real war is the war within our hearts, and it is a spiritual war. Events outside of us reflect events inside; divisions within the culture reflect divisions within individual hearts. The central fight each of us faces today is inside ourselves. It is a battle being waged between the forces of light and dark, between despair and hope. If hope can overcome despair, we live.

Living is more than continuing to breathe for another day. You can "die" today even while you go on plodding through your daily routines and fulfilling your responsibilities for another decade or several. You and I have both watched people who have given up their lives—forfeited their freedom and dreams and spirit—and have become little more than packages of habits and function. They are the living dead, and they show us an important truth. It is not the quantity of days that defines one's life but the quality of those days. We humans have the capacity for infinite suffering, loss of direction, and deadening of the spirit. We also have the capacity for fulfillment. We can experience satisfying and rewarding relationships, a sense of guiding purpose, affirmation of integrity, and deep meaning. When we surrender our lives to deadened routine in order to purchase security in an uncertain world, we die to that world.

Keeping Hope Alive

Do this: Understand that it is in your connection with others that you find strength. Nurture that connection to those with whom you have lasting commitment. Turn toward sources of information that are balanced and focused upon solid truth, not dramatic fact. Stay in the moment. Address the concerns of the present rather than the fears of the future. Look to supporting others rather than satisfying yourself. Seek constructive response rather than empty promise. Live the uncertainty. Keep the hope alive by taking action.

Expand your spiritual power. Instead of focusing upon division and blame, look instead at the implications of all religions. We are all riding a small rock through space, bound together by circumstance. We are each imperfect, and yet we each have within us a spark of the divine. Open yourself to the vast personal power that sparks promises. Find rituals, communities, and practices that grow the spark and allow it to glow in the dark. Share that universal connection with others who are frightened.

Rather than looking for unrealistic guarantees of security, develop your strengths. Explore the threads of meaning in your life that together form a cable bridging past and future. Look for themes, continuity, and promise within your own experience. Share what you are learning with others, and learn from their experience.

Use the strengths that brought us as a species through the millennia of threat and darkness preceding the comforts of civilization. The severest storms do not last forever. But as our ancestors have proven, resilient people endure. Use the power of understanding and community to keep on course through it all.

Gather Around the Fires

Our ancestors knew about being blown off course. They lived in constant danger and had to develop tools to deal with those threats. Historians point to the development of metal tools in the Bronze Age as starting the transition from living in the bushes to living in the high rise. Yet look again; it was the tools developed during the preceding period, by Neolithic hunter-gatherers, that allowed our predecessors to survive the carnivores and each other. The real tools of their culture were social. By banding together and sharing resources and lessons learned, primitive peoples survived their long night. Culture evolved through sharing, cooperation, and the spoken word.

The backdrop of uncertainty we now live with highlights and magnifies our personal struggles. The new age of anxiety: This is our desolate night of the soul. In the face of fear, threat, and confusion—through the tragedies and traumas of living in these times—we would do well to draw from our primal roots. Recall our two Neolithic ancestors who were attacked by a tiger. We can imagine how the survivor shared his story with his tribe members that night around the fire:

When he finished his account—partial and imperfect as it was—he thumped the talking-stick on the ground to signal that he was finished, at least for now, and handed it off to the next person. The others nodded and grunted assent and patted him on the back as he sat down. Or, maybe they didn't. Maybe they were stunned with horror and sat silently, contemplating tigers and the abyss. But we know that each of them took his turn with the stick. Some of them told new stories, and some told of what they had learned since they last spoke. Some retold their tales in ways that were different, fuller, more interesting. They all learned. And when the fire died down and the cold set in, they retired to their beds, taking with them the accumulated wisdom they had received. Their own stories merged with those of the others, and as the night moved on, the stories became dreams.

Recommended Reading

Books

Sheila Alson and Gayle B. Burnett. *Peace in Everyday Relationships: Resolving Conflicts in Your Personal and Work Life.* Alameda, CA: Hunter House Publishers, 2003.

Florence Bienenfeld. *Helping Your Child Through Your Divorce.* Alameda, CA: Hunter House Publishers, 1995.

Edmund Bourne. *The Anxiety and Phobia Workbook,* 4th Ed. Oakland, CA: New Harbinger Publications, 2005.

Martha Davis, Matthew McKay, and Elizabeth Robbins Eshelman. *The Relaxation and Stress Reduction Workbook.* Oakland, CA: New Harbinger, 2000.

Paul Foxman. *The Worried Child: Recognizing Anxiety in Children and Helping Them Heal.* Alameda, CA: Hunter House Publishers, 2004.

Kendall Johnson. *Classroom Crisis: The Teacher's Guide.* Alameda, CA: Hunter House Publishers, 2004.

Kendall Johnson. *Trauma in the Lives of Children: Crisis and Stress Management Techniques for Counselors, Teachers, and Other Professionals.* Alameda, CA: Hunter House Publishers, 1998.

Aprodite Matsakis. *I Can't Get Over It: A Handbook for Trauma Survivors.* Oakland, CA: New Harbinger Publications, 1996.

Daniel J. Siegel and Mary Hartzell. *Parenting from the Inside-Out: How a Deeper Self-Understanding Can Help You Raise Children Who Thrive.* New York: Jeremy P. Tarcher/Putnam, 2003.

Pnina Tobin and Sue Levinson Kessner. *Keeping Kids Safe: A Child Sexual Abuse Prevention Manual.* Alameda, CA: Hunter House Publishers, 2002.

Internet Resources

What Happened to MY World: Helping Children Cope with Natural Disaster and Catastrophe is a guidebook intended to help parents, and all those who work with families and children, during times of natural disaster.
http://www.mercycorps.org/topics/hurricanekatrina/publications
Jim Greenman, Mercy Corps 2006

Alcoholics Anonymous recovery program information is available on the web at:

http://www.alcoholics-anonymous.org/ and related twelve-step programs can be found by using the search keyword: 12-step.

Mental Health information abounds on the net; a reliable overview is provided by the National Institute of Mental Health at http://www.nimh.nih.gov/.

A great deal of parenting information is also available on the web. One reliable site with a great many links to practical information is KidsHealth: http://www.kidshealth.org.

Index

A

acknowledgment of responsibility, 205–207

action (during acute stress response), 134

acute stress reaction (ASR), 70, 73–76, 123; agitation, 128–129; anger management, 141–144; controlling, 129–134, 138; fear management, 145–148; grief management, 150–151; shutdown, 127–128; steps for intervening in, 130

addictions, 67, 91, 144

adolescents: need for independence, 177; stabilizing, 177–179; talking to after crisis, 170–176

"Age of Anxiety," 45–46, 47

agitation (acute stress response), 74–75, 128–129

alcohol, overuse of, 67, 133, 144

amends, making, 205–207

American Psychiatric Association (APA), 92, 94

anger, 61, 63–64; chronic, 137; and delayed stress reaction, 91; extreme, 137–138; plan for, 143–144; rage, 141–144; unresolved, 189

anger management, 141–144

angst, 57, 70, 108–109, 190

antidepressants, 54

anxiety, 54, 55, 61, 62–63; and acute stress response, 76–77; anxiety disorder, 93

apology, 206–207

appetite, loss of, 66

arguments, family, 180–183

arousal, symptoms of, 136–137

arousers (chemical), 72

art therapy, 194

attachments to the past, 165–166

attitudes: about loss of connection, 113–114; about loss of purpose, 112; about personal integrity, 114; about powerlessness, 113; shifts in, 68, 109–110

avoidance, 64, 95

B

behavior, changes in, 61, 67

beliefs, shifts in, 68

Bilsie, Ed, 153, 155, 164–165, 167

blockers (chemical), 73

bodily pacing (during acute stress reaction), 132

body awareness (during acute stress reaction), 133

body, rediscovering, 211

body therapy, 193–194

bombing, Oklahoma City Federal Building, 46

brain fade, 154

breathing problems, 53, 66, 132

burnout, 70

C

calm, creating, 69

Capacchione, Lucia, 195

change, personal reaction to, 60–61

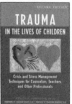

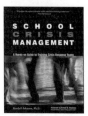

THE WORRIED CHILD: Recognizing Anxiety in Children and Helping Them Heal by Paul Foxman, Ph.D.

Anxiety in children affects their physical health and intellectual, emotional, and social development. Triggers include divorce, family breakdown, and a failing school system. The result? A shell-shocked generation of children who suffer from significant anxiety.

Dr. Foxman shows that this anxiety is preventable — or can be minimized. He explains the importance of rest, sleep, and exercise, and uses lists, exercises, sample dialogues, and case studies to outline steps that can be taken by parents, schools, health professionals, and children themselves.

304 pages ... 12 charts ... Paperback $16.95

DEALING WITH YOUR ANGER: Self-Help Solutions for Men by Frank Donovan, MAASW... Foreword by Allan Creighton

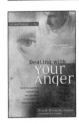

Donovan outlines a step-by-step procedure for reducing and eradicating anger. He explains how men can use the Emotional BioScan and the Personal Anger Monitor to identify and manage their emotions as well as to learn to de-fuel anger, recognize anger signals, and even put anger to good use.

272 pages ... Paperback $15.95 ... 2nd edition

PEACE IN EVERYDAY RELATIONSHIPS: Resolving Conflicts in Our Personal and Work Life by Sheila Alson and Gayle Burnett

As the world becomes — or feels — increasingly unstable, we must seek harmony close to home. We need the best possible relationships with families, friends, and coworkers. In this guide, two conflict-resolution specialists outline how we can negotiate the big and the small disagreements in our daily lives — with neither side feeling like a loser.

240 pages ... 1 illus. ... Paperback $14.95

KEEPING KIDS SAFE: A Child Sexual Abuse Prevention Manual by Pnina Tobin, MPA, and Sue Levinson Kessner, M.S.

The threat of sexual abuse is constant, and it is crucial to teach children how to recognize when they are in danger and how to obtain help. *Keeping Kids Safe* contains curricula for teaching kids ages 3–7 and 8–11 how to distinguish between wanted and unwanted touch, and to say "No!" and get help. A Facilitator's Guide discusses myths and facts about child sexual abuse, reporting procedures, and follow-up methods.

160 pages ... 31 photos, 3 handouts ...
Paperback $24.95 ... Spiral bound $29.95 ... 2nd edition

I CAN MAKE MY WORLD A SAFER PLACE: A Kid's Book about Stopping Violence
by Paul Kivel • Illustrations and games by Nancy Gorrell ... For children ages 6–11

This book shows children what they can do to find alternatives to violence in their lives. Kivel explains public danger (gangs, fights, drug-related violence) and private danger (sexual assault and domestic violence) and gives suggestions for staying safe. Activities and games are used to encourage readers to think about peace and justice, and the examples of Cesar Chavez and Julia Butterfly Hill are used to introduce activism. The drawings by Nancy Gorrell make the ideas easier to understand.

96 pages ... Paperback $11.95

ORDER FORM

10% DISCOUNT on orders of $50 or more —
20% DISCOUNT on orders of $150 or more —
30% DISCOUNT on orders of $500 or more —
On cost of books for fully prepaid orders

NAME

ADDRESS

CITY/STATE   ZIP/POSTCODE

PHONE   COUNTRY (outside of U.S.)

TITLE	QTY	PRICE	TOTAL
After the Storm		@ $14.95	
Classroom Crisis		@ $ 9.95	

Prices subject to change without notice

Please list other titles below:

		@ $	
		@ $	
		@ $	
		@ $	
		@ $	
		@ $	
		@ $	

Check here to receive our book catalog ☐ *FREE*

Shipping Costs
By Priority Mail: first book $4.50, each additional book $1.00
By UPS and to Canada: first book $5.50, each additional book $1.50
For rush orders and other countries call us at (510) 865-5282 extn. 301

TOTAL _____
Less discount @_____% (_____)
TOTAL COST OF BOOKS _____
Calif. residents add sales tax _____
Shipping & handling _____
TOTAL ENCLOSED _____
Please pay in U.S. funds only

☐ Check ☐ Money Order ☐ Visa ☐ MasterCard ☐ Discover

Card # _____ Exp. date _____

Signature_____

Complete and mail to:
Hunter House Inc., Publishers
PO Box 2914, Alameda CA 94501-0914
Website: www.hunterhouse.com
Orders: (800) 266-5592 or email: ordering@hunterhouse.com
Phone (510) 865-5282   Fax (510) 865-4295

ATS 3/2006